WITHDRAWN

People and Furniture

A Social Background to the English Home

MOLLY HARRISON

LONDON · ERNEST BENN LIMITED
TOTOWA/NEW JERSEY/ROWMAN AND LITTLEFIELD

*First published 1971 by Ernest Benn Limited
Bouverie House, Fleet Street, London, EC4A 2DL
and in the USA 1971 by Rowman and Littlefield*

© *Molly Harrison 1971*

*Book designed by Kenneth Day
Printed in Great Britain*

*ISBN 0-510-12521-2
USA 0-87471-037-5*

DA
115
H325
1971

I dedicate this book, with gratitude and
affection, to my husband. He shares my
interest in the mysterious influences
which determine, for all of us, the clothes
we wear, the furniture we choose and the
rooms we live in, and our 'disputations
about taste' have always been, to me,
enjoyable and useful.

... But after all that has been said by others,
or can be said here, no description of Great
Britain can be what we call a finished account,
as no cloaths can be made to fit a growing child;
no picture conveys the likeness of a living face; the
size of one and the countenance of the other
always altering with time. So no account of a
kingdom thus daily altering its countenance,
can be perfect.

Daniel Defoe, *A Tour Through England and Wales*, 1724

Contents

1 Perspective and Evidence   5

2 Before 1500   11

3 The Sixteenth Century   28

4 The Seventeenth Century   48

5 The Eighteenth Century   70

6 The Nineteenth Century   101

7 The Twentieth Century   129

   Glossary of Technical Terms   154

   A List of Books   155

   Acknowledgements   158

   Index   159

1 *Perspective and Evidence*

WHEREVER WE LIVE, whoever we are, our homes are very much a reflection of ourselves. What we buy, how we arrange our belongings, whether we keep them for a long time or renew them often – all this is a part of us, and it has always been so.

Furniture lasts longer than most other things in a house, and provides an intimate record, not only of changing fashions, but also of people's manners, habits, and even their views. How we sit, for example, is determined by the kinds of seats that are made for us – or that we make for ourselves – but those are, in turn, determined by our social habits. Look at these two chairs on page 7; they tell us a good deal about the very different ages in which they were made.

The modern chair is relaxed, comfortable, not made to last, likely to be quickly out of fashion, but eminently suitable for lounging and for sitting in all kinds of informal ways. The sixteenth-century oak chair is hard, stiff, very solid and long-lasting, but very uncomfortable. When most people sat on wooden stools, as they did in the sixteenth century, a chair was a mark of importance and the father of the household sat on it with dignity and pride. Comfort did not matter at all, but status mattered a great deal and one of its symbols was the possession of furniture.

In any case, comfort is a very relative thing. One's idea of comfort or discomfort is determined mainly by what one is used to: those who rode in horse-buses and those, later, who drove the early motor-cars were excited at many things, but comfort was not among them. Comparison, too, causes us all to consider comfort nowadays: we notice how much worse or better off our neighbours and friends are, and because of mass communications we know what other people, living in other parts of the country, have and use. The medieval peasant, on the other hand, was very little worse off than the small farmer for whom he worked, and his horizons were bounded by his village contacts. When life for everyone was hard and exacting, there was little to make people envious and dissatisfied. What we would call discomfort was normal, so it went unnoticed.

Until relatively recently the only furniture which survived was that which had belonged to well-to-do families. The rough, practical things, which were all the ordinary family had, were broken up and probably used as firewood when something more satisfactory could be got. None of them were worthy of special care, none of them were treasured as status symbols or as a form of investment and handed down from generation to generation. So it is inevitable that we know relatively little about how the ordinary family spent its life. Nobody thought it mattered much then; our century is the first to care about the condition of the common man.

Wealth and social position had much more influence in the past than now. Fine things were available for wealthy people, but others largely had to make do with what they could make themselves. It seems to us that there was dangerously little social conscience in earlier times, but of course that, too, is relative. Probably neither the designer of the elaborate marquetry chest-of-drawers on page 9, nor the wealthy, noble, family for whom it was made thought there was anything wrong in the inequality the piece underlined. Until recent times most men and women have known their 'station' and made the best of it. The furniture made then tells us as much about that as it does about the posture and the manners of those who used it.

New ideas spread slowly in the past, for until Gottlieb Daimler made the first motor-bicycle in 1885, no communication of any kind could happen faster than the speed of a horse or of a sailing-ship. Vice-Admiral Collingwood's Dispatch to the Admiralty announcing the victory at Trafalgar and the death of Admiral Nelson on 21 October 1805, appeared in *The Times*, in London, only on 6 November. This seems a fantastic thing to us, accustomed as we are to instant news and instant reaction. Similarly, a new fashion in chair or table, curtain or lampshade, can now be seen anywhere in the world on the very day on which it is first displayed to the Press. It is not surprising therefore that fashions change more quickly nowadays than ever before and that fewer and fewer people think of buying their furniture for a lifetime's use.

How do we know anything about our ancestors? What they looked like and what they used in their homes? Hearsay is always a poor guide and history books sometimes give contra-

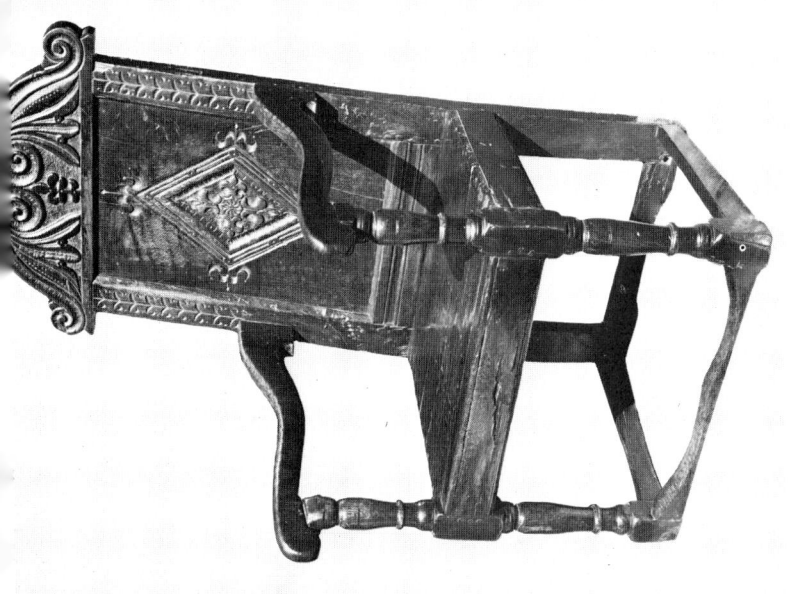

1 Hard and uncomfortable, but a mark of the importance of its owner, a chair of 1600

2 Relaxed, comfortable, not made to last, a chair of 1970

dictory impressions, according to the personal interests of the writer. It is more accurate, as well as much more interesting, if we can sometimes find first-hand evidence for ourselves. Where should we look?

We can find out about the clothes our ancestors wore from original garments in museums or in family chests, but also from drawings and paintings done at the time, from brasses, engravings, carvings, tapestries, and photographs. All these, recorded in paint, or line, stitch, or shadow, or print, can speak to us directly from the past, and if we use our imagination we can experience what it would be like to wear them.

Of course, people wrote about their clothes then, just as some of us still do now, and letters, inventories, diaries, and contemporary books can all give glimpses of what it felt like to be either a sixteenth-century merchant, an eighteenth-century nobleman's lady, or a nineteenth-century M.P. Such written evidence is, for most people, less vivid than the pictorial evidence and we remember what Queen Elizabeth I looked like from her many portraits, far more than from reading the fantastic inventory of her 4,000 dresses.

Furniture is inevitably less frequently depicted than faces and clothing, but sometimes we can catch a glimpse of a chair or a cupboard alongside the sitter in a picture, and occasionally workmen and their tools are shown in carvings and on small domestic objects. Some of the illustrations in this book are from such humble sources. But the real, solid, visual evidence about furniture of the past is in the actual pieces which have survived and which we can see and sometimes actually handle in museums, historic houses, and antique shops. Inventories and wills can tell us more about furniture than about costume – for obvious reasons – but always the thing itself speaks louder than any description of it. And it speaks more clearly and meaningfully if we have taken time to look closely, to compare, to discuss what we have noticed, and to read around the subject when we can. Even people who look upon period furniture as dull stuff, can feel excitement at the thought that when the chair in figure 1 was first brought home and the children told not to touch it or let the dog rub against it for fear of damaging the paint, anyone of the family could, if he walked far enough in the right direction, have talked to William Shakespeare. The thought can make the chair come alive in a very special way.

How accurate can we hope to be in visualising the past? We can never be sure, for it is indeed past – gone. But we can try to build up our own picture of what it was like to live in earlier times by combining our reading with our looking – whether looking at real buildings, furniture, and costumes, or at pictures of them. What we can never recapture is the feel and the smell of the past. No museum or historic house could possibly depict a period room accurately and keep any visitors, for the stench would be intolerable to modern noses. People rarely washed, laundry was an occasional exercise, dogs roamed indoors, refuse and mud on unpaved roads were a hazard not only to clothes but to rooms as well. Cleanliness, like comfort, is a very recent concern.

3   Elaborate marquetry cabinet of about 1690

Antiques nowadays tend to be highly regarded for three main reasons: some people find security in living among traditional things and form a sentimental attachment to Jacobean oak or Georgian mahogany, but not to modern pieces, however fine. Others, wanting very reasonably to find a safe investment and a hedge against inflation, fail perhaps to realise that the finest pieces of today will be valuable antiques tomorrow. And others, again, combine both purposes – personal security and financial hedge – and believe that a Chippendale chair is a status symbol, whereas a Marcel Breuer chair is not. As in everything, it depends on what you are looking for.

This book will not be concerned directly with any one of these considerations, but will try to look at English home life, and at furniture in particular, through the eyes of successive generations of men, women, and children. People are, after all, more interesting, as well as more important than things.

4 A medieval merchant, seated on a settle, counting his money on a table covered with a cloth. The influence of Church designs can be seen in the design

2 *Before 1500*

HUMAN AFFAIRS ARE ALWAYS CHANGING, but at some periods change is particularly slow and unpopular. The Middle Ages were such a time. For centuries English society had remained comparatively static, the Craft Guilds dominated all workmanship, and thought had been directed by Church authority. No man could hold or express views different from those of Mother Church; if he did he was a heretic and acted at the peril of his body in this world and of his soul in the next.

Medieval society gave most of its thought to satisfying religious needs. So much wealth was in the hands of religious institutions that it is not at all surprising that the Church was the chief patron of the arts and the source of new ideas, even in domestic surroundings.

The first furniture was made by masons for the Church, and it is in churches and cathedrals that it can still be seen. Very little of it has survived however, for in our damp climate wood is particularly liable to rot.

Even wealthy houses were cold, damp, dark, and draughty and were scantily furnished. Materials were limited; although there were dense forests in many parts of the country, oak was needed for building ships and houses, and there were frequent times of scarcity when demand outran supplies. The simple tools which were available – axe and adze, gouge and drill – were not suited to quick or fine workmanship, hand manufacture was a very slow process, and change in design was rare. Furniture lasted for many generations.

Carpenters were the craftsmen responsible for all large-scale uses of timber, such as house-building, shipbuilding, and fortification. They became experts in timber; building was their chief business and we can still marvel at their skill when we see the roof of Westminster Hall which has a span of 67 feet, and the hammer-beam roofs of East Anglian churches. Medieval carpenters were so proud of their skills, and of the part played by carpenters in the Bible, that Noah and St Joseph, at work with their adzes, were portrayed on the walls of Carpenters' Hall, in London.

Fashion played a relatively small part in the furnishing and equipment of the medieval home; life was precarious and dangerous, and people of all social levels felt, understandably, that security was more important than anything else. When your home might be attacked without warning, and when you might at any time have to flee from plague or pestilence, you did not want to encumber your family with many possessions, even if they were available. Mobility was your first consideration.

Much early furniture was structurally dependent on walls and built like cabins along the sides of the great hall. 'Standing' pieces were relatively rare.

The well-to-do classes were much influenced by continental taste, and imported some of their furniture from Flanders and France. The word 'foreign' had little meaning; Europe was, to medieval people, divided into nobles, freemen, and peasants, rather than into Englishmen, Frenchmen, and Burgundians. The concept of nationalism as a major force was still two hundred years ahead. The Church, too, was a strong unifying influence and Latin and French were international languages, spoken by cultivated people throughout the Holy Roman Empire. We can therefore get a fair impression of furniture in England in the late Middle Ages from religious paintings and from illustrations in French manuscript books of the time, such as that on the opposite page.

In the early Middle Ages there were no separate rooms even in wealthy households, and everyone lived, ate, and slept in the same room. Families were often large and the smaller homes must have been very crowded; the larger ones needed a great many servants and the people who lived in a castle or manor-house were almost as many as would live now in a small village. With so many people and so few rooms there could not have been any privacy in your home, whether you were rich or poor.

Later in the Middle Ages, with a gradual increase in material goods, people began to be more concerned about privacy and the hall was no longer the only room in a large household. Gradually, smaller rooms were added round it: a kitchen, a buttery and pantry, a sitting-room called a 'solar', and separate bedrooms. The inventory of heirlooms at Stonor, in Oxfordshire, in 1474 mentions: a hall 'y-hangyd with blacke saye [serge]'; a little chamber in purple and green; four

5 A curtained bed, built-in seating, and a stool by the fire. Evidently a well-to-do burgher's house

chambers in red and green; the chamber 'at nether end of the hall' which was 'hangyd wyth grene worstyd'; and a 'parlour chamber' which was particularly well equipped with 'blankettes' and 'schetes' and a 'ffedur bedde' and so was probably the principal bedroom. There is also mention of a buttery, kitchen, and bakehouse. A fifteenth-century merchant's house in King's Lynn had a great many rooms, including a 'counting-house'.

These smaller rooms were less public places than the all-purpose hall had been and so it was less important that the floor space should be kept clear. Because of this, furniture began gradually to lose its connection with the wall and became free-standing.

We know little about the personal possessions of the poorer classes, for they could not write and so left no diaries or letters, could not afford to have their portraits painted, and often had nothing to leave in a will. There are, however, a very few inventories of simple folk; in the mid-Essex records there are occasional references to peasant households, and what strikes us as strange is that there is mention of tubs, barrels, vats, troughs, and other utensils for making food and drink, but hardly ever of anything that can be called furniture. They only had what they made themselves and this was so rough that it served for a limited time only and was thrown away or burned for firewood when the impoverished owner died. On the other hand, equipment for cooking – rough but serviceable – was virtually indestructible and was passed on from generation to generation.

Chests

The earliest, most important, and most widely used article of storage furniture was the coffer or chest. The coffer was smaller, often covered in leather, and essentially portable; both were usually fitted with strong and elaborate locks and there was nothing else in which you could keep the few belongings you had.

The first kind of chest was made from a length of hollowed-out tree-trunk, strengthened by bands of iron to prevent it from splitting. A slice cut off the top served as a lid, and in remote parts of the country such pieces of furniture continued to be made until the seventeenth century. More of them have survived in parish churches than in private houses; there are good examples at Wimborne, in Dorset, and East Grinstead, in Sussex.

Here is an extract from a church inventory of 1464:

> item in the lowe house under the vestry   ii old iron bound coofres
> item in the vestrye   i gret olde arke to put in vestryments
> item in the house afore the Chapter hous   i old ire bond cofre, having hie feet and rings of iron in the endes thereof to have it by. And therein lieth certain bokes belonging to the Chapter.

The rounded top of the hollowed-out chest or 'coofre' prevented it from being used for anything more than storage, and when such chests were listed in private inventories, it is reasonable to assume that the household was wealthy and not obliged to use one piece of furniture for several purposes.

The next stage of development was the planked chest – a wooden box made of six boards nailed or pegged together – and, later, the framed chest, consisting of a framework into which were fitted thin rectangular panels. Sometimes the panels were plain, sometimes carved, and often coloured. The members were fitted together by mortise and tenon joints and by wooden pegs, called 'dowels'.

All the early chests stood directly on the floor and there was continual risk of damage from rats and from the wood rotting through contact with a damp floor of earth or rushes. The 'hie feet' referred to in the inventory above were a convenient protection against this. An enterprising carpenter had evidently thought of making a chest with its side pieces longer than the height of the front and back.

The carving of these early pieces of furniture is very similar to that made by the masons who were carving the stone decoration in churches at the time. In fact, a good deal of domestic furniture was still inevitably made by masons, who were equally skilled at working in stone and in wood. Woodcarvers also developed their own individual forms of decoration and, of these, the 'linenfold' was the most popular. This was a formalised representation of cloth hanging in vertical folds. It may have been used originally on linen chests, or on those in which documents were kept, for some versions of linenfold look something like scrolls of parchment. These 'parchment panels' as they are sometimes called, were used to decorate walls as well as furniture.

Flat-topped chests were used as seats, ranged along a wall, perhaps with strips of fabric on their lids, also as storage for clothes, tools, armour, and other valuable possessions, and for servants to sleep on. Coffers were used as safes and as suitcases, portable ones were called 'trussing coffers' (the word being used in the earlier sense of 'packing'), those not used for travelling were 'standing coffers', or 'standing chests'.

So many coffers were arriving in England from the Duchy of Burgundy in the late fifteenth century that the English arkwrights (arc or coffer-makers) protested to Parliament that this was harmful to their trade, and the traffic was prohibited by an Act of 1483. However, some people evidently managed to evade the law, for 'Flanders Chests' are mentioned in household inventories quite late in the sixteenth century! (The Low Countries were possessions of the Dukes of Burgundy.)

Other Storage

A pole, or perch, for hanging up clothes is shown in a scene of the Nativity of St John the Baptist, in the *Holkham Bible Picture Book* in the British Museum. Pegs hammered into the wall were an alternative.

6 A fifteenth-century game of draughts. Notice the linenfold panelling on the settle, the chest, and the food cupboard

Food was kept in an aumbry, or press, a kind of cupboard on long legs with the doors pierced for ventilation. Because bedrooms were so cold it was the custom to have a snack during the night, or on waking up, so a ration of beer, bread, and wine was often kept by the bedside. These rations were called 'liveries' and later the aumbries were called 'livery cupboards'. It is interesting to note that the word no longer has any connection with the food or provisions given to guests or to servants, but is used to describe the uniform or badge provided for the latter. Not everyone approved of the medieval habit of having snacks during the night, and Thomas Tusser, in the early sixteenth century, condemned the custom in a book entitled *Five Hundred Points of Good Husbandrie*

> some slovens from sleeping, no sooner be up
> but hand is in aumbrie, and nose in the cup.

As more wealth was spent on domestic comforts and luxuries it became fashionable to show off the family plate, and furniture was becoming a matter of prestige. At first a simple side-board was used for this purpose and a late medieval English romance refers to 'the cupboard with plate shyning fayre and clere'. The buffet or dresser was a grander development: the buffet was a stand of open shelves, often with a closed cupboard underneath.

The exaggerated extent to which buffets were considered as indicating prestige and status, at high social levels, is shown in a book *Les Honneurs de la Cour* written by a Frenchwoman who was much concerned with etiquette. She explained that buffets for ladies were to have two shelves only, countesses could have three, princesses four, and queens five. The cloths draped on the buffets were similarly regulated. This seems ridiculous to us, but we must remember that during the Middle Ages there were stringent sartorial rules also: trade and industry were supported by rules concerning who could wear this or that fur, how many yards of wool had to be used in a skirt, and so on. On paper, at least, they were a disciplined lot.

Seating

The window-seats so often shown in medieval illustrations imply that there was a great scarcity of movable seating. They were often of stone, hard, upright, and cold, and again we are reminded that comfort mattered little and that life was dangerous. You were quite likely to be knifed in the back if you sat in the middle of the room at a time of feud, so it was safer against a wall, and by the window. It was lighter by the window, too, for the only artificial lighting was by rushlights and candles, and these must have been very hard on the eyes.

The hall of a medieval house was a busy, crowded, place, and its floor space had to be kept as free as possible, and furniture out of the way. While the dais, or raised section, was a permanent feature at the end of the hall, members of the household and important guests were seated on a bench there, facing the rest of the company. The 'chair' on which the lord of the manor sat was often nothing more than the elaborate centre-piece of this fixed bench.

At the end of the fifteenth century movable chairs were still a rarity, and in rich houses there was usually not more than one, used solely by the master of the household as a mark of his status; other people sat on chests, benches, or stools. All early chairs were *arm*chairs, upright symbols of rank and power; the sitter sat *up*, nobody ever sat *back* or *down*.

In early medieval times 'chairs' and 'thrones' were interchangeable terms and even as late as 1548 the town council of Lyons, in France, stipulated that an elaborate piece of work ordered from a local goldsmith should be decorated with the figure of 'a king seated upon a chair'. Even in much later times chairs were reserved for honoured guests and there are frequent references, in letters and diaries, to people being affronted and their status impugned when they were offered a stool, and not a chair to sit on.

The practice of giving a chair only to the most important visitor has long passed away in Europe, though it persists elsewhere. The custom has, however, survived in our language, as customs often do: in a university it is only a professor who has 'a chair', and 'Mr Chairman' has the ultimate authority in any gathering.

A very usual kind of seating was a bench, made as part of the framework of the walls of a room and, in reality, just a narrow ledge. Stools were more convenient, for they were small and easily portable. Early manuscripts often show rulers sitting upon foldstools and these must have been particularly convenient for abbots and bishops who, as well as royalty, were likely to be moving continually from place to place.

A settle, or bench with a low back, was an economical arrangement for mealtimes and probably evolved from fixed pews in churches. Sometimes, there was a carved panel in front, probably intended to keep feet and legs away from draught. In the British Museum, among a set of medieval chessmen, the piece representing the king has a chair with a solid half-back and small solid side pieces.

Two rare types of chair are known to have been in use in the Middle Ages: those with X-shaped frames were probably the more comfortable. Turned chairs with rush seats we think of as being eighteenth-century 'Windsor' types, but evidence shows us that they were not unknown in the mid-fourteenth century.

Some early chairs are shown fitted with foot-rests, probably as a health precaution, to keep the feet off the floor. The floors

7 Jan Arnolfini and his wife, by Van Eyck. An idea of household furnishings of the time is given by the carpet on the floor, the mirror, the chandelier, and the bed with its knotted curtains

of even noble households were strewn with rushes which were rarely changed, and mingled with the mud from men's boots, the filth of dogs, fragments fallen from the table, and bones thrown down. Cleanliness, as we understand it, was not a great concern for medieval families and it is not at all surprising that so many children died in infancy. There are no reliable statistics from which we can estimate the number who died young, but there are many examples recorded of large families of whom few grew up. Many monumental brasses and tombstones show a whole row of boys and girls who died before their parents, and we know that Dean Colet, Headmaster of St Paul's School in London, was the eldest of twenty-two children, but was the only one who lived to be thirty years old.

Tables

Tables were at first long boards resting on trestles, such as we see in paintings by Pieter Brueghel. They could be put up quickly if unexpected guests arrived, and dismantled to give extra space after a meal. At Penshurst Place, in Kent, there is an oak table, 27 feet long, which has been in use there since the end of the fifteenth century. It is a 'fixed' table, not on trestles, and would have stood on a raised dais across the upper end of the hall, for the family and their guests, while the servants sat at smaller tables, lengthwise down the hall.

In well-to-do homes the table was frequently covered with a linen cloth, on which were set out spoons and knives, cups and jugs made of wood and of earthenware. Royalty and high Church dignatories used gold and silver dishes. Plates were often of wood, and frequently meat was eaten off trenchers, or thick slices of bread, which were afterwards given to the poor or flung on to the floor for the dogs. Forks were not used in England until the seventeenth century, but were known before then as an Italian affectation.

A section in John Russell's *Boke of Nurture*, a book of manners produced in the late fifteenth century, shows us clearly how much rearrangement of tables and seats was necessary after a meal:

> ... the removal of the Table and separate Service to grand guests in the Chamber, it is instructed ... thenne uprysying, servitours muste attende to avoyde [clear away] tabills, trestellis, formys and stolys, and to redress bankers [benches] and quyssyons [cushions].

8 A fifteenth-century banquet. The furniture is plain, and the picture shows a royal canopy, a buffet, and sparse table-ware

A table was called a 'board' for obvious reasons and the word had a wide variety of additional meanings. When it was said that someone had a 'plentiful board' the visitor knew that he would be fed well; the 'cup-board' was a shelf used for the display of plate when one's wealth, and the assumed honesty of servants and visitors, made such display possible; a 'side board' was a side-table – only a distant ancestor of the piece which we call by that name. There are several ways in which the word 'board', meaning at first a plank of wood, has spread into our language: boarding house, board-and-lodging, board room, board table, board of governors, boarder, boarding school. One remnant of the early meaning of the word has nearly disappeared; but over the doors of some of the oldest London schools you can still see the letters S.B.L. – School

9 A settle used as a bed, with a hanging to keep off the draught, a stool, and some cooking utensils can all be seen in this picture from a fifteenth-century manuscript

Board for London. The erstwhile 'Board of Education' has long since gone, and only very occasionally does one hear an old man or woman refer nowadays to the 'Board School'.

Beds

Beds were a great luxury in medieval times and the sleeping arrangements show us vividly how difficult it must have been to keep warm, even if you were well-to-do. In medieval pictures of bedrooms people are often shown naked, but it is likely that, in reality, most people slept in their day clothes in winter, for warmth.

For hundreds of years people slept on benches, settles, or chests. Peasants, servants, and children lay on straw pallets, or bags, of dried ferns, rushes, or heather, placed along the sides of the walls or grouped round the fire in the centre of the room. The first beds were built against a wall and were structurally

22

part of the building. A canopy or 'tester' hung from the ceiling and the bed was enclosed by thick curtains, making it in effect a room within a room. During the day-time the bed curtains were knotted, so that they would be out of the way, and from some illustrations it appears that they were then used as bags in which to store possessions not in day-time use. The mattress was supported on ropes threaded through holes in the bottom framework.

Originally, the word 'bed' applied to the materials upon which people slept, whether there was an actual piece of furniture or not. In *The Reeve's Tale* Chaucer refers to a miller who made up a temporary bed for two guests:

> Again, and in his chamber made a bed
> With clear white sheets and blankets fairly spread.

The miller and his wife very evidently had the only proper bed in the house, for

> Ten foot from his, upon a sort of shelf
> His daughter had a bed all by herself

So valuable was a bed at this time that it came to be reckoned as one of the most important items of a man's estate. In 1392 Richard, Earl of Arundel, paid his second wife what we might consider to be a doubtful compliment, in leaving her in his will 'A blue bed marked with my arms and the arms of my late wife.' This custom lasted a long time, for in Shakespeare's will he left, as a bequest to his widow: 'My second best bed with the furniture.' Presumably by then the term 'bed' included the bedstead as well as the bedding, and the 'furniture' consisted of the mattress, covers, and hangings. A nobleman moving from manor to manor might well take his bed – as well as the panes of his window glass – with him.

A 'box-bed' was one enclosed by wooden panels on three sides, with curtains which were drawn across the open side, to make a cosy little room. Servants often slept near their masters or mistresses in case of danger, or a need for service during the night, and they used a low bed, called a truckle- or trundle-bed, which had small wheels at the corners and was pushed – trundled – under the bigger bed during the day-time. In *The Merry Wives of Windsor*, Falstaff's room at the Garter Inn is described thus: 'There's his chamber, his house, his castle, his standing-bed and truckle-bed.'

Babies were tightly swaddled and laid in cradles made of wood, plain or carved according to who made them, and often there was a hood to keep out the draught, and large rockers.

Cradles, like beds, were objects of prestige as well as of comfort and use. In a fifteenth-century manuscript on *The Christening of a Prince or Princess* there is mention of a need for two cradles, one for use in the nursery, the other, larger and more richly decorated, for display on ceremonial occasions.

Important persons received their guests in bed, which was certainly warmer and more comfortable than sitting on a hard-seated, high-backed, chair. Making a royal bed was an important ceremony which was carried out by two yeomen of the bedchamber, instructed by a gentleman usher. The yeomen had to tumble about on the bed and plunge a dagger into it, to make sure there was no danger there.

The *Babees Book*, a book of etiquette and good manners, written in the late fifteenth century, instructed a young man in the duties connected with the care of his master's bedroom:

> Then return in haste to your lord's chamber, strip the clothes off the bed and cast them aside, and beat the feather-bed, but not so as to waste any feathers, and see that the blankets and sheets be clean. When you have made the bed mannerly, cover it with a coverlet, spread out the bench-covers and cushions, set up the head-sheet and pillow, and remove the basin. See that carpets be laid round the bed, and dress the windows and the cupboard with carpets [tapestries] and cushions.

Soft Furnishings

Rich men invested money in tapestries which, with carpets, were the status symbols of an age when constant travelling meant that valuable possessions must be easily carried about. By 1500 the great houses of England were full of hangings imported from Flanders and from north-eastern France, particularly from the town of Arras. So 'the arras' came to mean 'the curtain'. The various words used to describe hangings for beds, walls, and chairs were all of Norman-French origin: tester, banker, dosser, and coster.

Those who could not afford tapestries hung painted cloths

on their walls for decoration, to exclude draughts, and to give an impression of warmth and colour.

Cushions were stuffed most frequently with horsehair or fur; 'down' cushions were those stuffed with moss and were thought to be inferior in quality. Upholsterers were forbidden by the rules of their Guild to fill their mattresses and cushions with goat's hair because of its powerful and unpleasant smell.

Reading and Writing

Chaucer's Clerk of Oxenford had books by his bed, probably in a small chest, but apart from scholars – both lay and religious – books could only be bought by the wealthy. They took so long to write and illustrate, and were so precious, that they were classed with silver and gold plate, and with jewels, in wills and inventories. Most medieval books were religious ones: Bibles, devotional works, and lives of saints; but there were technical books for doctors, lawyers, and administrators;

10   A monk seated on a folding stool, his writing slope standing on a chest. Notice the writing equipment, a drawer, and rush matting

romances for courtiers; chronicles, guide-books, and many books of etiquette. The learned books were in Latin, the courtly ones in French and, from the beginning of the fifteenth century, books in English became more and more common. In 1475 William Caxton printed the first book in English, and from that time books began to be much less expensive, much less bulky, easier to read, and so available to a far wider public. There was, however, little furniture made specifically for reading or writing until the next century.

Chests were sometimes used as writing-tables; illustrations in manuscripts show us monks and scribes writing at desks which are merely sloping boards, and ladies on window-seats reading.

Most women had neither time nor, probably, any inclination to read, but in noble and wealthy classes there must have been a large number who were literate, for the private accounts of royal households contain many entries referring to the purchase of ABCs and writing-tablets for the princesses, and of books for the queen and her ladies.

In medieval Europe, up to the end of the fourteenth century, letter-writing was a task left almost entirely to professional scribes and lawyers. In England, however, during the fifteenth century, it became fashionable for men and women in established families to write their own letters, and to write them mostly in English. Several collections of fifteenth-century family letters and papers have been preserved: those of the Pastons of Norfolk, the Stonors of Oxfordshire, and the Celys of London and Calais all give us a vivid impression of a cruder and rougher, but simpler and fresher, world than that of today. This was a time of growing national feeling, and as wealth and personal security increased, and the amenities of life were more easily obtainable, men and women began to question accepted religious teachings, to read of new thoughts and theories, and to look for new ways of equipping their homes. The Renaissance was in the air and before long its influence was to show in domestic furniture and furnishings.

11 This illustration from a medieval manuscript shows the interior of a house, with a window-seat and a desk

3 *The Sixteenth Century*

SOME DAYS, SOME YEARS, some periods seem to contain not only the seeds of new thought and new feeling, but the leaf and flower and fruit as well. Such a period was the sixteenth century. The Renaissance had come late to England, via France and the Netherlands, after its springtime growth in fourteenth-century Italy. In the reign of the first Tudor, Henry VII, the new ideas influenced scholars and the king's court; by Shakespeare's day they had reached the people. It was a busy and exciting time in which to live, a time of great change in manners, in social life, and in standards of comfort.

Even the English countryside was being altered; the open fields of the Middle Ages were now enclosed by ditches and by hedges of nut trees, hawthorn, crab-apple, and sloe, and even simple families living in remote districts felt and saw that change was afoot.

People's ideas about themselves were changing too. In the Middle Ages everyone knew his place and very few people became much richer or poorer than their parents had been. Now, fortunes might be won and lost and power was moving from the aristocracy to the merchant class.

Venice had stood at the heart of the old Europe, midway between East and West, but her power had declined as the Turks blocked the traditional trade routes. The legacy of Venice passed to Antwerp, and then to London, whose merchants were ready to expand their trade. The discovery of America was to make the Atlantic no longer a frontier, but a highway, and England was becoming the geographical centre of the world, as well as the financial centre of Europe.

The dissolution of the monasteries, which began in 1536, also had its effect upon domestic life. When the monks were ejected, their movable property, such as plate, jewels, and furniture, went straight into the royal coffers and had little further influence upon fashion. The craftsmen who had worked in the monasteries were also dispersed and so their skills were at the disposal of new patrons with new ideas, and the medieval Gothic influence upon woodworking gradually disappeared.

The early printing-presses had a startling and rapid effect

upon people's lives. Men were becoming dissatisfied with the old ways of thinking and wanted to work their ideas out for themselves, and this began to happen just at the moment when these ideas could be spread more quickly and effectively than ever before.

Even the map of the world was changing, for countries were being discovered which had not been heard of before. The discovery of the New World must have been as exciting for them as space travel is to us. Young Englishmen were finding wealth and adventure in trading and fighting on distant shores, and the wealth and goods they brought home increased the prosperity of townsman and countryman alike. Ambitions were soaring and the new prosperity led to greater comfort in the home for all but the very poor.

Building

Englishmen were great builders during the sixteenth century. The most striking difference between the new houses and those that had been built during the Middle Ages was that the earlier ones had been designed primarily to repel visitors and the later ones to accommodate them. By 1500 the moat, which had previously been essential for safety, was little more than an ornament. The portcullis became a porch, with sometimes a friendly motto carved over the door, as at Montacute House, in Somerset:

> Through this wide opening Gate
> None come too Early none
> Return too late.

Grand houses were built in stone, often imported from Italy, and other houses in brick. The character of smaller houses depended upon local conditions and the materials available, for roads were still very bad and it was costly and difficult to carry materials from one part of the country to another.

Most houses were still timber-framed, with the spaces in between the beams filled in with laths and plaster. Bricks were mainly imported from the Low Countries, so that in eastern England many new houses had brick filling in between a timber framework. In stone districts, such as the Cotswolds, Wales, and some parts of the North, houses were solid and austere, with walls of stone and roofs of stone or slate. Elsewhere roofs were of thatch or clay tiles.

In 1587 William Harrison, writing in *A Description of England*, commented on the changes in building materials:

> The ancient manours and houses of our gentlemen are yet, and for the most part, of strong timber, in framing whereof our carpenters have beene and are worthilie preferred before those of like science among all other nations. Howbeit, such as be latelie builded are commonlie either of bricke or hard stone, or both. . . .

Great attention was paid to symmetry of plan, and larger houses were often built round a courtyard. Early in the century chimneys were still rare and great houses had very tall brick ones, richly patterned. All new houses of any standing had glass windows, in place of the horn or oiled linen ones of medieval times. Windows were so large and so numerous that Francis Bacon wrote that it was sometimes impossible to get out of the sun or out of the draught! There were no architects in the modern sense of the word. For a grand house the plans were often drawn up by a master mason. He and his workmen built the shell of the house; the master carpenter was responsible for internal details such as ceilings, walls, and staircases. The owner would contribute new ideas as the building progressed, so that the result was often a startling mixture. Building was often very slow and many houses changed character before they were finished. Smaller houses must often have been built by the owner, with the help of friends. A licence from the Lord of the Manor was needed in order to be allowed to build on common land, as this letter of 1598 to the Lord of the Manor at Fornham All Saints, in Suffolk, shows:

> Sir – Thomas Rodger the younger; an honest true labouring man in his trade of plowright . . . hath made his humble suit that we would in his behalf be humble suitors to your worship that it might please you to give him licence to built himself up a cottage or poor dwelling-place upon a piece of the common next the east end of your pasture. . . . But because many have interest of common in that plot of ground . . . the poor man fears he shall not get all their consent before your worship's good liking thereof may be had. And to the end that your worship may be advertized whose consents are already given, and who they be that humbly sue in his behalf – the underwritten have severally subscribed name or mark . . . [11 signatures follow]

12 A sixteenth-century version of *Christ in the Carpenter's Shop*, showing St Joseph at work with the adze. One of a set of wall-paintings in Carpenter's Hall, London

Rooms

Early in the century the chief room was still the hall, as it had been in the Middle Ages. Gradually, however, larger houses were built with a 'long gallery' on the first floor. This was the chief room for the family and was like a long corridor, with windows all along one side. Increasing wealth gave people an opportunity for greater privacy; instead of dining publicly, great men now took their meals in a dining-room built for that purpose; for carrying out their estate business they had a parlour, and sometimes even two – one for winter and the other for summer use. The solar became a sitting-room, and bedrooms were becoming separate from other rooms.

Of course, not every home had all these rooms, and even in a well-to-do house the hallway might still contain a bed, and the parlour often did so. Farmhouses and cottages were usually only one room deep; for the majority of people bedrooms, or 'chambers' as they were called, were partitioned with wood and one led out of another, without a passage.

Dr Levinus Lemmius, a Dutch visitor to England, wrote in praise of English rooms in 1560:

... the neate cleanliness, the exquisite finenesse, the pleasaunte and delightfull furniture in every poynt for household, wonderfully rejoysed mee; their chambers and parlours strawed over with sweete herbes refreshed me; their nosegayes finely entermingled wyth sundry sortes of fragrante floures in their bedchambers and privy roomes, with comfortable smell cheered mee up and entirelye delighted all my sences. . . .

Hitherto, fashion had been largely restricted to clothes, armour, jewellery, the patterns on fabrics and on silver and gold vessels; but now fashion began to influence the shape and decoration of everything used in the houses of the wealthy.

Walls

The stone and timber-framed walls of medieval interiors had been left bare, except for movable tapestries to give warmth and colour. The Flemish fashion of lining the walls with framed woodwork, or wainscot, came only slowly to England. In 1516 Erasmus visited the Bishop's Palace at Rochester, in

13 *Visiting the Poor* by Pieter Brueghel the Younger. The furniture is sturdy but primitive, and the picture shows an interesting variety of household equipment, including a settle, a cradle, and even a baby chair

Kent, and found that 'the walls of brick and mortar exhale noxious vapours' and afterwards he wrote to suggest to His Lordship that a wainscoted room in the Palace would be much better!

In Elizabeth's reign William Harrison wrote:

> The walls of our houses on the inner sides be either hanged with tapisterie, arras worke or painted cloths . . . or else they are seeled with oke of our owne, or wainscot brought hither out of the east countries, whereby the rooms are made warme, and much more close than otherwise they would bee.

This extract shows that 'wainscot' referred to foreign oak; the process later called 'wainscoting' was at first known as 'ceiling' the walls of a room.

The tomb of King Henry VII in Westminster Abbey, made in 1512 by an Italian, Pietro Torrigiano, had a great influence on English craftsmen. Woodworkers began to use the new Renaissance designs and we can see the Italian influence on woodwork in the richness of detail in Christ Church, Oxford, the Great Hall at Hampton Court, and the choir-stalls of Henry VII's Chapel in Westminster Abbey.

Walls and mantelpieces were among the first domestic features to be made in the new style, and furniture soon followed. Linenfold-carving was no longer high fashion and now surfaces were broken up with pilasters, cornices, and carvings of human and animal forms. The craze was for all things 'Italianate', whether appropriate or not. But these new fashions, many of them copied uncritically from the pattern books which were brought to England from the Continent, were alien to the English tradition. Not all craftsmen, or all patrons, understood Antique art or Classical architecture and much decoration was mishandled by woodworkers who were not really in sympathy with the new trends. The taste of the new rich mercantile classes had a coarseness and lavishness which, to our eyes, are typical of the mid-Victorian taste of three hundred years later.

Floors

The floors of the downstair rooms of simple cottages consisted of bare earth beaten down hard. More comfortable homes had floors of boards and these were strewn with rushes and sweet-smelling herbs which laid the dust and muffled some of the noise.

Erasmus, who did not enjoy his visit to England as much as Dr Levinus Lemmius had done, ascribed the plague – from which England was hardly ever free – to

> the incommodious form and bad exposition of the houses, to the filthiness of the streets, and to the sluttishness within doors. The floors are commonly of clay, strewn with rushes, under which lies unmolested an ancient collection of beer, grease, fragments of bones, spittle, excrements of dogs and cats, and everything that is nasty.

Instructions in *The Young Childrens Book*, written in 1500, and now in the Ashmolean Museum in Oxford, show us that attempts were made to train children in clean habits, then as now:

> Caste not thi bones ynto the flore,
> But ley them fayre on thi trenchore.

Carpets, brought to England from Persia and India, were at first hung on the walls, or laid across tables and chests, but seldom laid on the ground except on very special occasions. When Queen Elizabeth visited Nonsuch Palace, in the apartment where she was to give audience 'the floors were strewn with straw and hay, only where the Queen was to come out and up to her seat were carpets laid down'. Fine-quality carpets, placed on tables or buffets as a background to gold and silver plate, were called 'borde' carpets; more ordinary ones that could safely be walked on, but were still very scarce, were called 'ffote' carpets.

Plastered ceilings came into use to prevent warmth from escaping through boarded floors above. An urge for display transformed the useful into the ornate, and plasterwork in fashionable homes was either painted or decorated with raised patterns. Much of this 'pargetting' was also applied on the outside plastered walls of merchant and yeoman houses, as we can still see in many East Anglian towns and villages.

Fireplaces

The central fire was no longer fashionable; as soon as brick, stone, or plaster was used for walls there was much less danger from fire, and wall fireplaces replaced the open hearth in most new homes. The smoke went up a chimney instead of drifting round the room, and the indoor air was much cleaner. It then became fashionable to leave furniture its natural colour and to wax and polish instead of painting it. The beauty and variety of its colour and marking began to be appreciated, and surfaces were treated with beeswax or with turpentine obtained from the resin of conifer trees. In Germany and the Low Countries, where large, enclosed porcelain stoves had long been used for heating rooms, furniture had gleamed with polish for generations before this became acceptable in England.

Beds

The piece of furniture that is referred to most often in wills and inventories of the sixteenth century is the four-poster bed, which had gradually replaced the box-bed surmounted by a tester fastened to the wall. William Harrison, writing in 1577, commented on 'the great amendment of lodging, for our fathers, yes and we ourselves also, have laid often upon straw pallets, on rough mats covered only with a sheet, and a good round log under their heads instead of a bolster or pillow'.

14 An oak truckle-bed on wooden wheels, with holes for the ropes which supported the mattress

Grand beds often had elaborate hangings of crimson velvet or cloth of gold, or yellow or purple silk, and the inventory of Lord Lumley's possessions drawn up in 1590 shows us an incredible richness of furnishings. At Lumley Castle there were five gilt bedsteads, twenty-three bedsteads of walnut or marquetry, and another forty of oak. It would be for this grand type of *ménage* that these instructions to a valet were laid down in *The Book of Nurture* by Hugh Rhodes in 1568:

> When your master intends to bedward, see that you have fire and candle sufficient and see that you have clean water in at night and in the morning and if your master lie in fresh sheets, dry off the dankness by the fire; then fold down his bed and warm his nightkerchief, help off his clothing and draw the curtains.

There were no springs in mattresses, which were laid on wooden boards or else on ropes threaded across from one side of the framework to the other. On top of the wool mattress all but the poorest had a feather-bed, blankets, sheets, and an embroided counterpane. Such beds were handed down from generation to generation and were prized possessions.

They were no longer intended, as box-beds had been, to stand out of the way in a corner. As houses acquired more rooms, there was space to show off your bed and it was given the most prominent place, not along a wall but against it and projecting into the room. Often the new type of bed was richly carved, as we can see on the Great Bed of Ware in the Victoria and Albert Museum; the tester was supported by the four posts and no longer hung from the ceiling, and the curtains too were hung from the frame of the bed.

Truckle-beds were still much used in simple homes. Cradles were important pieces of furniture everywhere and grand ones were covered with silk or velvet. The more ordinary were of carved oak and often had the baby's initials carved on the end. The baby was bound into its cradle with its swaddling-bands and often there were large iron staples along the sides, or holes bored through them, into which the swaddling-bands were threaded. Sometimes there were knobs on the side to keep the bedding in position.

There was evidently such a demand for beds early in the sixteenth century that dishonest tradesmen used unsuitable materials in the making of them, and regulations had to be

15 A sixteenth-century chest, unusual both in shape and construction

laid down forbidding the use of mixed materials in pillows and mattresses: '... because by the heat of a man's body, the savour and taste is so abominable and contagious, that many of the King's subjects thereby become destroyed'. The proclamation added that 'For their own use, however, and not for sale, persons might make or do to be made, any of the aforesaid corrupt and unlawful wares.'

The demand for beds was not fully met by the carpenters and joiners, for we read in inventories of the mid-sixteenth century of such dual-purpose pieces as 'a long settle with a bed' and 'a settle with a mattress upon it' and 'a settle with a bed'. It is obvious that the distinction between a bench and a bed was still a very fine one.

Storage

For centuries, no one invented a way of locking things away safely, except in a chest.

After the end of the Wars of the Roses, people gradually began to feel confidence in the stability and power of the Tudor monarchs and the ordinary family began to find new material security. For 'top' people, however, the times were still intolerant and dangerous, religious and political power were closely entwined, and not many paces separated the Council Chamber from the block, as the story of Sir Thomas More in *A Man for All Seasons* reminds us.

But, once public affairs were more stable, homes were more secure and people felt a need for more varied pieces of furniture for private purposes.

There is an extensive vocabulary of terms to describe the new storage furniture. Our knowledge of what people possessed and used is mainly *verbal* — we read of furniture in wills and inventories, but it is difficult to relate what we read to existing pieces we can see in museums and antique dealers' shops. An aumbry, a hutch, a press, a buffet, a court cupboard, a livery cupboard, a cupboard-chest: all these were in use during the sixteenth-century, some seem to be interchangeable, yet at the time each must have had a specific meaning. Writers tended to change their use of terms as frequently as they changed their spelling! Inventory-makers of the time referred frequently to the number of doors and shutters which enclosed some of the compartments in the varied pieces of storage furniture. A list of 1567 refers to 'an almerye with iiij doores . . . a presse . . . with v doores' and so on, almost as if the number of doors was the chief distinguishing feature between one piece and another.

Here is a popular ballad, written in 1547, which tells us of some of the ways in which people were spending their new wealth. There were no banks, so it was not always easy to know how to use extra money:

> For they that of late did sup
> Out of an ashen cup
> Are wonderfully sprung up;
> That nought was worth of late,

Hath now a cupboard of plate,
His table furnished too
With plate beset enow
Parcel gilt and sound
Well worth two hundred pound.

16 A carved open court cupboard of oak, for the display of plate

Chests, which for centuries had been virtually the only storage furniture, declined in importance as people began to want more convenient pieces. The chest had always had one great handicap: it must have been almost impossible to keep the contents tidy, for they were inevitably piled one on top of the other. The first attempts to adapt the chest to new ideas and new requirements were the invention of thoughtful joiners sometime during the sixteenth century, and it soon became customary to keep things in small boxes or 'tills' inside a chest, so that everything of a sort could be kept together. This meant, however, that if what one wanted was near the bottom of the chest, several boxes had to be lifted out. So the next improvement, sometime towards the end of the century, was to do away with the front panel of the chest and pull, or *draw* the little boxes out along specially made grooves, instead of lifting them. Little knobs on the front of each box made the whole process easier and in time they came to be called 'drawers'. So the chest had become first a chest-with-drawers and then a chest-of-drawers, such as we know today.

Seating

Frequent references in wills and inventories to a 'a set of six stooles' shows us that these were still widely used. They were the normal seating at dinner-tables, and were also used as tables for small children, who sat on low stools.

17 A cheerful child in a sixteenth-century German baby chair

The typical sixteenth-century chair was in essence a box with solid back and arms added, and was called a 'box-chair'. It was made by a joiner, of native oak, and reflected the qualities of that timber: weight, strength, and rigidity. If you are splitting a log of English oak, it cleaves almost straight, because of the vertical lines of the grain, so all early oak furniture was basically rectangular. The tools were still very simple, so the mortise and tenon joints were rough and the carving not elaborate.

At first the seat of the chair could be lifted up and things kept inside; then people began to find that this was inconvenient and carpenters started to make chairs without boxes. They still had panelled backs, but were fitted with legs joined together by 'stretchers'. The legs and stretchers were the last vestiges of the framework of the earlier box-chair.

In an inventory of 1556, the contents of Sir William More's bedroom at Loseley House, in Surrey, were listed:

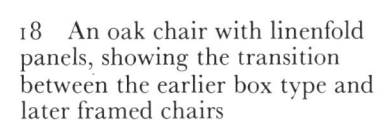

18 An oak chair with linenfold panels, showing the transition between the earlier box type and later framed chairs

In the Chamber wherein I lye . . . a joyned bed, a lyttle joyned chayre, another joyned chayre, iiij joyned stoles of chestnuttree for women.

Such a chamber usually also contained a chest for valuables, placed at the foot of the bed and serving as a seat, and a second one for clothes and linen.

A back-stool was simply a stool fitted with a back; it was not at first thought of as a chair because it had no arms, and until the late sixteenth century a chair proper always did have arms. Later the back-stool was called a 'single-chair' or 'side-chair', to distinguish it from the chair with arms, which came to be called an 'arming chair' or 'armchair'.

Back-stools were first made during the middle years of the sixteenth century, when ladies wore wide farthingale skirts which took up a great deal of room. Later they came to be called 'farthingale' chairs. A poem *The Patient Countess*, published in 1587, refers to 'a stoole half-backed with a hoope' which was offered to the gentleman guest by a cottager.

The box-chair was certainly not intended for comfort, but when once comfort became a major consideration and furniture began to be made as much for ease as for show, many changes were introduced into seating. Among the first modifications to the traditional box shape was the raked back, sloping slightly. The legs were still straight and it is surprising that these chairs did not topple over, until we remember that they were so heavy that they were difficult to move.

Perhaps it was the habit of some masters of some households to lean back so far that their chairs tilted (then, as now!) and even fell over, which encouraged joiners to think out another improvement: quite often these early oak armchairs have their back legs thicker at the bottom. This, and stretchers placed almost at ground-level, helped to make the chair more stable. The 'box' shape is still evident, but it is gradually being modified.

Arms sloping downwards, often with scrolled ends, were another step in the direction of comfort and a relaxation of posture. A glance at the costume of the period reminds us that a woman would have been unlikely to sit in a chair of this kind, even if she wore unfashionably narrow skirts, for she was tightly corseted and would find any position, other

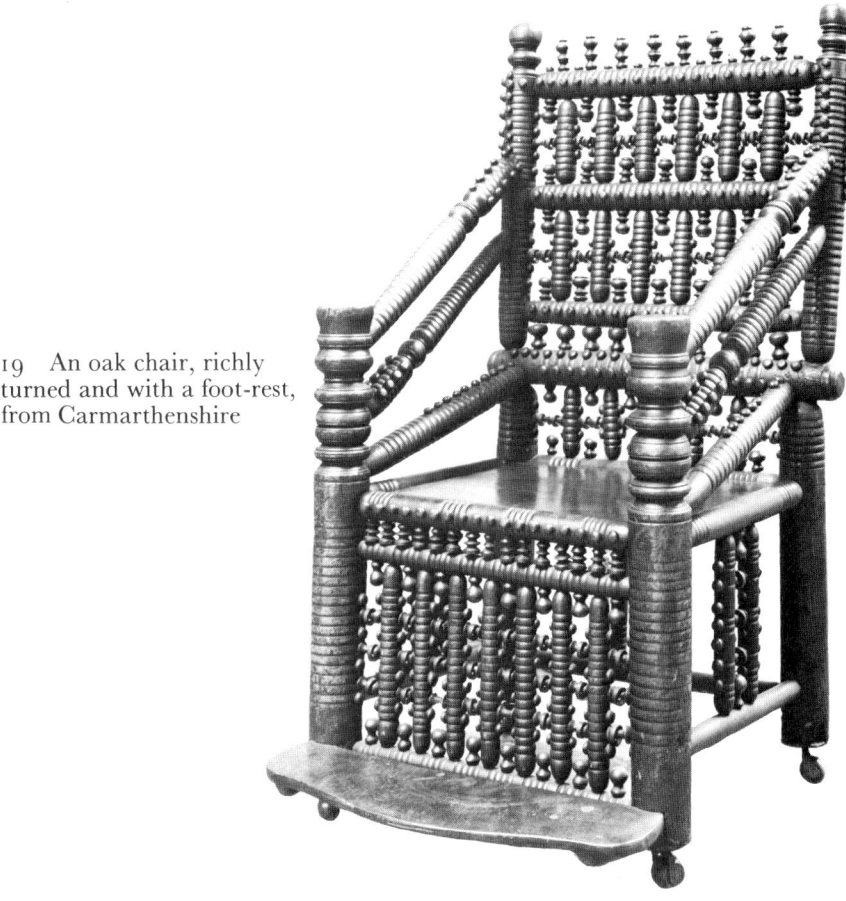

19 An oak chair, richly turned and with a foot-rest, from Carmarthenshire

than a rigidly upright one, both uncomfortable and unseemly. The changing shapes of chairs were for the benefit of those who paid for them and used them – the men. During the sixteenth century, turners, too, were seeing new ways of developing their historic craft in satisfying the requirements of well-to-do 'rising' customers. They were granted a Charter in 1600, which must have given them new status and confidence, for they began to have a marked influence on furniture design. On chairs, as well as on buffets, court cupboards, and table legs enormous bulbous turnings were fashionable. An elaborately turned chair is shown above.

The increasing role of women in social life had a marked effect upon the design of seating. By the early sixteenth century many upper-class women had achieved enough independence to be allowed to enjoy social occasions on their own, without their menfolk being present. There is an engraving by Abraham

Bosse, which shows a recently delivered mother being visited in bed by her friends. They are sitting round the bed on light, movable chairs which are very different from the heavy box-chairs still in use. A 'woman's chayre' is referred to in an inventory of 1547, but these light, portable seats were also known by their French name – *caquetoires* or 'gossip' chairs.

'Close-stools' or 'secret stools' were in use indoors by wealthy families, though the majority of people used the age-old earth closet outside. We need to remember that nobody, however wealthy, enjoyed any form of water-supply. In 1579, in Tower Street, in the Parish of All Hallows, London, among the houses of sixty wealthy merchants there were, according to the parish records, only three privies. At Knole, in Kent, there was reference at this time to 'a square box with a lifting lid, covered in velvet, held in place by gilded nails, and the top quilted for comfort'.

Tables

Although long, heavy tables with six or eight legs, like the one at Penshurst, were made throughout the sixteenth century, they were used only in grand houses and in the dining-halls of colleges and of city companies. They are described in inventories as 'long tables' – the term 'refectory table' is modern.

Other people, becoming accustomed to the greater privacy of smaller rooms, needed smaller tables which could, if necessary, be used for larger company. The concept of an extending table, or 'drawing table' was an entirely new one, thought up by some inventive joiner whose name we do not know. We do know, however, that by the end of the century they were not uncommon, for a merchant in Newcastle upon Tyne had 'drawing tabills of waynskot'.

The drop-leaf table, with single- or double-hinged leaves supported by folding arms or hinged gate-legs, was another ingenious space-saving device. In the dining-parlour the table did not have to be moved after a meal to make room for other purposes. It stood in a permanent position in the middle of the room and acquired a dignity and importance it had not had before. However, in *Romeo and Juliet* (1597) the servants are instructed to clear the hall and 'turn the tables up' for dancing.

Small, light tables were made for other purposes than dining, and there is mention in inventories of several kinds of small table: square, rectangular, round, hexagonal, and octagonal. Sir Thomas More wrote of 'a small tabill in the chamber wherein I lye', which was presumably a bedside table. Horizons were widening indeed.

Decoration

Everything made by man is an expression of the mood and flavour of his time. Even those people who appear to be ahead of popular taste at any moment are expressing a more widely felt urge for change. This spirit, or stamp, of a period shows itself in detail and ornament as much as in the buildings, furniture, and clothes.

The two qualities characteristic of sixteenth-century England were a new appreciation of comfort and an inordinate love of display and decoration. Exuberance in dress and manners matched exuberance in architecture and interior decoration. Elizabeth's reign saw the increase of new 'risen' families based on sheep-farming, and they wanted to express and display their new wealth.

Not everyone approved of the new love of ostentation. Ralph Stubbes, in *An Anatomie of Abuses* denounced the widespread custom of displaying armorial bearings on houses or

20 *(opposite)* A woodcut of 1525 shows a very simple table and benches

furniture, as showing the vice of pride:

> Everyone vaunts himself, crying with open mouth, 'I am a gentleman, I am worshipful, I am honourable, I am noble; my father was this, my father was that; I am come of this house, I am come of that.'

Medieval furniture had invariably been painted, probably as a preservative. By the sixteenth century painters had risen to the status of artists and were inclined to consider that decorating the work of craftsmen was beneath their dignity. So much of the furniture decoration which would previously have been done by painters was now left to woodworkers instead.

Carving was lavish; upon many pieces of grandiose furniture there were elaborate carved floral or architectural motifs, or free-standing sculptured figures; and inventories of relatively modest families frequently refer to carved cupboards, bed-posts, and buffets.

During the mid-sixteenth century a decorative device called 'strapwork' was introduced into England from Antwerp and this soon influenced the decoration of woodwork, including furniture. This was a *drawn* form of decoration, illustrated in the many copy-books brought to England by workmen from the Low Countries, and not an idea worked out in three dimensions as, for instance, linenfold had been.

Inlay, or marquetry, had been known in Classical times, but had not been much practised in medieval Europe. Because of Church influence painting, gilding, and carving had appealed more to medieval taste, and these crafts had been used in domestic interiors also.

Now, in the sixteenth century, inlay became high fashion. It was made 'in the solid'. That is, the background wood was hollowed out to a depth of about a quarter of an inch, to receive shaped inlays of other woods – apple, cherry, pear, or bog oak (black oak). These decorative pieces were, literally, 'laid in' the surface of the piece.

The 'Nonsuch' chest in the Victoria and Albert Museum is typical of many inlaid pieces. The name 'Nonsuch' arose because the buildings depicted in inlay on the surfaces of the chest were based on the designs for Henry VIII's famous Palace of Nonsuch, near Cheam in Surrey.

More expensive materials than wood, such as ivory, ebony, and marble were also used for inlay. A late sixteenth-century draw table at Hardwick Hall in Derbyshire was described in an inventory of 1600 as 'inlayde with marble stones and wood'. An elaborate cabinet made at about the same time and now at Stourhead in Wiltshire has inlaid ornaments in amber, sapphires, emeralds, and semi-precious stones. This would not, of course, have been in any way typical.

William Harrison was one observer who deplored the new extravagance and ostentation which, he thought, were having a softening effect upon men's characters. In 1577 he wrote:

> For, when our houses were built of willow, then had we oaken men; but now that our houses are come to be made of oak, our men are not only become willow, but a great many among us altogether of straw.

21 *Lord Cobham and his Family* by Hans Eworth. Notice that even small children were dressed like their parents; there is pewter table-ware, a rushlight, and household pets

4 *The Seventeenth Century*

IN THE HISTORY OF EUROPE the seventeenth century is often referred to as the 'intellectual century'. And in England too, it was an age of great debate and of religious and political tension and strife.

The first two Stuart kings believed they were rulers by divine right, but the country gentry and prosperous merchants, who had gained new status as a result of the commercial prosperity of Elizabeth's reign, were pressing for a say in the government of the country. The king was still expected to meet the ordinary costs of government from his own purse, but this was a period of inflation and rising prices and both James and Charles tried to levy special taxes to meet their expenses. These efforts, and much gross extravagance, were resented by Parliament, and an impossible constitutional situation led inevitably to civil war.

The country was split in two by a criss-crossing of loyalties: Royalist versus Parliamentarian, Churchman versus Puritan, old gentry versus rising merchants; the north and west of the country versus the south and east. Friend found himself against friend and families were bitterly divided.

Oliver Cromwell was a genius as a military leader, but as Lord Protector he exercised an authority stricter than most English kings had ever wielded. His government was a military dictatorship, but extremism of any kind has always been detested by Englishmen. At his death in 1658 the country was threatened with anarchy until, in 1660, the bells rang joyfully and 'the world of England was perfectly mad' at the accession of King Charles II.

The Restoration was welcomed, not only by faithful Royalists, but also by all those who wished to put a stop to armed strife. Charles II had lived on the Continent during his exile and inevitably brought back to England many fashions from the French and Dutch courts, and many foreign craftsmen. He was a keen patron of both art and science.

Many of the disturbances of this century were caused by religious differences. It was an intolerant time and those who did not accept the doctrines of the Established Church had to endure much hardship. Persecution directed against both Catholics and Puritans was so severe that many of them fled the country and established settlements across the Atlantic.

During the Commonwealth the Puritans in their turn were relentless in their persecution of others. Charles II himself was tolerant and tried to stop religious fanaticism, but without much success. Men of all viewpoints had many old scores to settle, superstition was still rife, and witch-hunting commonplace.

The late seventeenth century was a time of many-sided intellectual activity; it saw the foundation of the Royal Society, in which courtly wisdom and enthusiasm, academic thought, and practical scientific experience were brought together. The physical sciences, trade, agriculture, navigation, and discovery, the science of banking, and the arts of building and decoration – all were constant topics at the endless committee meetings to which the court and city men gave so much of their time.

In spite of religious and political troubles, these were prosperous times. The new colonies meant wealth and power for merchants, for the noblemen who were sent to administer the new settlements, and for English society as a whole. It was a time of warm-hearted, lavish enjoyment of civilised living; much of the new wealth was spent on houses, furniture, and gardens, though there were a great many families still living in simple cottages, with little furniture and no comforts.

Building

Early seventeenth-century England was faced with a severe timber shortage, as the woodlands were cut down for firewood and shipbuilding. Timber soared in price and regulations were passed restricting the use of wood:

> There hath been such consumption of timber in the Realm that in the very City of London they are now driven to build with beech and other timber of small continuance which in time will be the notorious peril and decay of the city. It is now commanded that no part of a tree that may serve for any use of timber shall be converted to coal or firewood; and . . . no one shall erect any new house, or the forepart of any house . . . except all outer walls and windows be made of brick, or brick and stone.

22 *A Cottage Interior* by Jan Steen. There are simple chairs, a trestle table, and a cane cradle

The new brick houses were strongly influenced by the ideas of Inigo Jones who, after visiting Italy and studying Classical buildings, had designed the 'Queen's House' at Greenwich in 1616. This is symmetrical, both in plan and in elevation; each part is balanced by the other parts and each measurement – the size of the windows for instance – has a mathematical proportion to all the others. Inigo Jones, in fact, composed a new style, the English Renaissance style. Most of his work was for public buildings, such as the Banqueting House in Whitehall, but he also designed houses for his friends and these, in turn, influenced other private houses both large and small all over the country, though first in the south and east.

The fear of fire, following the Great Fire of London in 1666, was another reason for the increased use of brick. The new houses were very plain, with sash-windows symmetrically placed, broad wooden glazing bars, a hood to give importance to the central doorway, a horizontal band between the ground and first floors, and a bold cornice. Streets of regular, terraced brick houses of this type became the basic pattern for London and other towns for the next hundred years. Larger houses in the country were built with similar restraint and simplicity.

Rooms

The plan of the new houses was simple. The entrance hall usually opened through an arch into the staircase hall; there was one living-room on each side of this, with bedrooms on the first floor. This was reached by the richly carved staircase which had now become an important feature of the interior.

The walls of the main rooms were covered with larger panels than previously. These were of oak or pine, unpainted, and in fashionable homes they often served as settings for portraits by Van Dyck, Lely, and minor painters. Less wealthy families had their portraits painted by artists who travelled about from house to house in the country, staying for a few days where they worked.

Stucco ceilings were exuberantly decorated, chimney-pieces elaborately carved, and profuse swags carved in lime and other woods added richness and gaiety to grand interiors. Embroidery and tapestry brought lavish colour to the walls of many rooms; carpets on floors were still rare, but woven rush matting provided more hygienic and up-to-date covering than the earlier strewn rushes. In the account book of Knole, in Kent, there is reference to a purchase, in 1624, of 'six pairs of matts to mat chambers with at thirty yards apiece'.

During much of the century, furniture continued to be made of oak in the traditional way, varying in style from one locality to another.

The main political events were reflected in furniture; heavy and richly carved at the beginning, during the ponderous, autocratic reigns of James I and Charles I; austere and simple during the Commonwealth; lighter, frivolous, and much more varied in purpose after the Restoration. But we must remember that communications were still so slow and primitive that even war or revolution in one part of the country had relatively little effect in another. Among the letters written in

1640 by Lady Sussex are some which deal with buying carpets: 'one woulde bee very fine for a bede' and another would 'not suet with my hanginges and chers', and we sense that her concern for minor domestic matters is in no way disturbed by the likelihood of civil war. Hers was not, as ours is today, a world of instant news.

Seating

The battle between dignity and comfort continued and gradually dignity was the loser. Chair seats had occasionally had fabric fixed to them in the sixteenth century, and loose embroidered or tapestry cushions had doubtless for long been used on stools when the lady of the house had time and inclination to make them, or to have them made, but this was not upholstery.

Perhaps nobody had thought during the sixteenth century of padding chairs because their clothes were themselves so well padded that the hard seats caused little discomfort; but in any case it is significant that a concern for padding furniture occurred at about the time that men's padded nether garments began to go out of fashion! Early in the seventeenth century Sir John Harrington complained of the hard stools he had to sit on at court, compared to the 'easy quilted and lined forms and stools to be found in every merchant's house'.

At this time chair seats and backs were, in grand establishments, fitted with fixed padding: velvet, brocade, 'Turkey work' (a form of embroidery which incorporated carpet knotting), satin, and wool were used as covering materials, and the padding consisted of wool, hair, or oddments of waste fabric.

A famous set of upholstered chairs of the early years of the century are those in the Brown Gallery at Knole, which were made for the State visit of King James I to the house in 1604. These are oak chairs, with every part of the woodwork covered with brocade, velvet, and damask coverings – even the legs! This was an exaggerated style, unusual even for its period, and suggesting that the host and hostess were somewhat overwhelmed at the honour paid them by the new king.

Chair-making was becoming a distinct craft, combining the skills of joiner, carver, turner, and upholsterer. Provincial

23 An upholstered X-chair at Knole, beside a portrait of Lord Sackville seated on one of the same set

24 An oak chair, padded and covered with 'Turkey' work

craftsmen were, of course, very little influenced by London fashions in furniture; they continued to work by habit and custom and only made pieces of familiar design and construction, so that a great deal of early seventeenth-century furniture looks very like sixteenth. Box-shaped, joined, chairs are listed in many inventories and were still reserved for the master of the house and his guests.

John Osburne, a yeoman of Writtle, in Essex, whose goods and chattels were listed in 1683, kept:

> In the Hall – one great joyned table, eight stooles and one forme 1 li. 10s.
> one little joyned table, 2 stooles and one great joyned chayer 8s.
> one cubbard and one settle with 3 boxes in it 1 li.

Robert Jackson of Writtle possessed, in the same year:

> In the Hall – one table, 2 formes, one joyned stole 1 li. 6s. 8d.
> 1 bench bord, 4 cushens 13s.

In the Porler – one joyned bedsted with all that belongeth to it   5 li.
2 chayers, 1 little table and one joyned stole, one cuberd, 1 warming pan   1 li. 15.[1]

The simple pieces owned by John Osburne and Robert Jackson were of a type which lasted a long time in unfashionable parts of the country, and which would have appealed particularly to men and women of Puritan tastes. The eleven years of Cromwell's rule did not last long enough to set a specific furniture style. This is a pity, because what remains of really early American furniture shows us that the Pilgrim Fathers took with them joiners who could make simple, very beautiful, Puritan pieces.

Although leather was not used for upholstery before the middle of the century, it played a part in domestic interiors long before that time. 'Sling' seats for X-chairs had sometimes been made of leather in the sixteenth century, and leather 'carpets' for covering beds and tables, and leather folding screens, are mentioned. At Ham House, Richmond, Surrey, there is the only known example of a leather 'carpet', forming part of the seventeenth-century furnishings of the Queen's Room. It was discarded sometime in the eighteenth century, as not being in the current taste, and was found in the attic of the house only a few years ago.

There was a long tradition of covering chests and coffers in leather, and the same technique began to be used to cover chair seats and backs. These chairs were described as 'covered all over, garnished with nails' – the leather was fixed to the carcase of the chair with brass-headed or gilt round-topped nails, arranged in a regular pattern and the leather was sometimes tooled or painted.

A List of Household Stuff in 1614 mentions:

> ... a cowche of crimson leather, painted border wise with silver and golde, one long and two short cushions suteable to the same, linedn with bayse couloured velvets and laced about with gold lace.

Such a couch would have had a back and two ends; the term came from the French word *coucher*, 'to lie down', and one of the medieval terms for a bed was a 'couche'.

---

[1] 1 li. = 1 livre = £1. And notice that spelling had not been standardised even as late as the seventeenth century.

The day-bed was a long seat, very like a couch but usually with only one end, either fixed or adjustable by means of a ratchet. Although people of all classes were anxious to make their homes more comfortable in whatever ways they could, there was still a certain amount of contempt for comfort, as having a softening influence. Shakespeare's Richard III is spoken of praisingly by the Earl of Buckingham when he says: 'This Prince is not an Edward! He is not lolling on a lewd day-bed!' The current view was that if you were in bed you were either asleep or ill; if you got up you were expected to be about your business.

The need for day-beds, for those who did want to 'loll', became less as chair-makers began to pay more attention to comfort; and to make lighter, more portable, and more subtly shaped pieces. In the new chairs the arms sloped downwards and were curved; the seat was lower and much more comfortable; the carved top rail, or cresting, was usually made to rest on the uprights of the back instead of being held between them; the legs had barley-sugar twist or bobbin-turning; turned stretchers were high off the ground; the short and straight back gave way to a longer, shaped one. Gradually the chair ceased to have any visual affinity with the box shapes of the previous century.

A material which competed with upholstery to give added comfort and mobility to chairs was woven canework, introduced into England from India and China in the second half of the seventeenth century. This consisted of palm canes split into thin strips and interwoven to form an openwork mesh. Of course, as always happens in such situations, there were indignant protests from upholsterers and from makers of woollen cloth, who saw in these changes a threat to their interests. In 1680 the cane-chair makers presented a petition to Parliament in which they stated:

> ... that about the Year 1664, Cane-Chairs etc. came into use in England, which gave so much Satisfaction to all the Nobility, Gentry, and Commonalty of this Kingdom (for their Durableness, Lightness, and Cleanness from Dust, Worms, and Moths, which inseparably attend Tirkey-work, Serge and other Stuff-Chairs and Couches, to the spoiling of them and all Furniture near them) that they came to be much used in England, and sent to all parts of the World.

25 A day-bed of carved walnut and cane. Notice the barley-sugar turning and the painted panel

Oak was too heavy a wood to be used in conjunction with canework, so beech, another native wood, was used instead for the new, light, cheap chairs. This wood was not wholly satisfactory, however, as we can see from this extract from *Sylvia* by John Evelyn. The 'timber' whose shortage he was bemoaning was oak:

> Were the timber in greater plenty amongst us, we should have far better utensils of all sorts, as chairs, stools, bedsteads, tables, wainscot, cabinets etc., instead of the more vulgar beech, subject to worm, weak and unsightly.

Chairs now began to be made in 'sets' – two armchairs and half a dozen, or more, single, armless ones. Dr Claver Morris, a successful doctor who lived in Devonshire, noted in his diary for 1686 that he bought one and a half dozen 'Turkey-work chairs' and 'ten leather chaires'. So chairs had become plentiful and, as Dr Morris probably needed a large number for the musical evenings which he so much enjoyed, he bought a set, although their style was rather old-fashioned. Living in Devon, he probably did not know or care much about new fashions.

High-chairs were made for children in any suitable wood; they had long legs and a movable bar across the front. The baby 'cage' or go-cart was a piece of nursery furniture which was intended to help small children to walk. It was rather like a skeleton skirt made of wood, with a hoop for support under the arms, and small wheels fixed to the lower part of the frame. This seems to us a dangerous way of teaching a child to walk, but we must remember that floors were far from clean, a baby's clothes long and elaborate, and laundry an occasional, ceremonious affair.[1]

Settles were still much used in country districts. They had high or low backs and were fixed or free-standing, but now often had a locker or drawer under the seat. Gradually the

[1] In the laundry of a great house a huge wash was done every three months or so and took several days. Soap was made from a mixture of fat and ashes dissolved in water. At Haddon Hall, Derbyshire, there is a wooden washing 'tally', measuring $5\frac{1}{2}$ inches × $4\frac{1}{2}$ inches, with fifteen squares each marked with the name of a piece of clothing, and with a dial under it numbered from 0 to 12 – very much like the movable notices people put out now to tell the milkman how many pints to leave.

26 A small girl in a go-cart, pushed by her elder sister. Detail from *A Family Group* by Coques

27 A wooden doll of the late seventeenth century, beside a clumsy miniature oak chair. The doll is 15¾ inches high

settle became a less rigid piece, with upholstered seat, curved back, and lower arms. By 1700 it had become the settee.

Storage

The Great Fire of London of 1666 destroyed thousands of houses and their Elizabethan and Jacobean furniture. Masons, joiners, carvers, and metal-workers flocked to London from the provinces and abroad, to find work in the reconstruction. Guild restrictions were relaxed because of the crisis, and new materials, new designs, and new techniques were eagerly discussed. Those who rebuilt and refurnished did so in a very different style and with a new wood – walnut.

Walnut, imported from France and Italy, was widely used for the remainder of the century. At first, like oak, it was used for pieces of solid construction, but there was increasing interest in the natural markings and colouring of timber and in a new technique of manufacture which could show these off to advantage. This was 'veneering'.

28 Woodcarving of a joiner's shop. One man is planing, the other is turning a bulbous table leg on the lathe

Veneering consists of cutting very thin sheets, called 'veneers', of figured wood or of some decorative material such as ivory or ebony, and gluing them on to the specially prepared flat surface of a more common wood. The purpose in making pieces in this way was in no way to fake or hide the construction, but to use the qualities of two different kinds of wood in conjunction: a suitable, cheaper, readily available wood such as deal, for the carcase, and an equally suitable, but more decorative, expensive, and rare wood such as walnut for the surfaces. The new technique was developed just at a time when people's hopes and ambitions were growing. Change was in the air and domestic items which had formerly been thought of as luxuries were now regarded as necessities by anyone who could afford them. More and more, new furniture was wanted for storage.

The old style of chest or coffer continued to be made until the end of the century, but its use gradually declined, even in country districts. The chest-of-drawers, which had evolved from the chest, was usually veneered in walnut, or inlaid, and had its use in many varied rooms in a well-to-do home. Some chests-of-drawers rested on a stand, and a fashionable but very inconvenient piece of storage furniture, called a 'tallboy', was in effect one chest-of-drawers upon another.

Towards the end of the century wealthy homes were furnished with a wide variety of cupboards and cabinets. Owing to the popularity of two new social customs – tea- and coffee-drinking – fashionable people began to collect Oriental porcelain, which they liked to display in a china-cabinet with glazed doors. Small corner cupboards with glazed doors were also used for displaying porcelain, and these were often built into the panelling of a room.

Queen Mary, wife of William III, was an enthusiastic collector of porcelain and in the Water Gallery at Hampton Court Palace corner fireplaces were topped by shelves to hold favourite pieces, and cabinets were specially built for her Delftware. John Evelyn refers in his diary to a grand supper-party he attended, at which 'all the vessels which were innumerable, were of porcelain, she is having the most ample and rich collection of that curiosity in England'.

China-cabinets to hold valuable collections were not made by joiners, but by specialists who called themselves 'cabinet-makers'. By the beginning of the next century the term 'joiner' had been dropped, and from that time 'cabinet-making' has been used to describe the making of all kinds of furniture, and 'joinery' refers to rough woodworking.

Evelyn, in his diary, referred to the high standard of English craftsmanship at this time:

> Locksmiths, Joiners and Cabinet-makers and the like from very vulgar and pitiful artists are now come to produce works as curious for the fitting and admirable for their dexterity in contriving, as any we meet with abroad.

Until the Civil War, the average man did little writing. The few who could, did all their writing at their place of business; if they had any reason to write at home they certainly would not have a piece of furniture specially for writing.

After the Restoration, changing habits and widening interests led to a demand for many kinds of reading and writing furniture. The development of trade offered better employment to men who were literate, and many merchants found it necessary to have a piece of furniture in their homes at which they could write and do accounts.

Small desk cabinets had tiny drawers for letters and documents, often the legs had a delicate barley-sugar twist and the stretchers were curved; larger, more solid cabinets had mirror doors and drawers in the lower part, and towards the end of the century bureaux were fashionable. These had several drawers and a sloping lid which could be let down on pull-out supports for writing. A bureau-cabinet and a bureau-bookcase were fashionable combinations of two different pieces, and a 'scriptoire' was a small writing-cabinet with a fall front.

A fair proportion of ordinary people could read and write by now. Some of them made up their accounts, wrote love-letters and business letters, and kept diaries both in shorthand, like Samuel Pepys, and in longhand. But people who were not wealthy found it difficult to lay hands on books and would certainly not own a bookcase.[1]

It was at this time that pieces of furniture began to be fitted with pull-out slides for supporting candle-sticks. Bureau-bookcases nearly always had one or two slides below the bookcase section, and a candle burning in this position gave a good light to the writing space. The doors of bureaux were often fitted with sheets of mirror to reflect the light of the candle.

The earlier court cupboard, also called a 'buffet', was no longer a piece on which plate was displayed to impress visitors, but had become a receptacle for storage in the dining-parlour. In her *Tour Through England on a Side Saddle*, written at the end of the century, Celia Fiennes described a room with 'a neat booffett furnish'd with glasses and china for the table, a cistern below into which the water turn'd from a cock, and a hole at the bottom to let it out at pleasure'.

Nearly all these large pieces of 'case' furniture were made of imported yellow deal, suitably prepared to take veneers, or marquetry. Marquetry is a very advanced form of veneering – a kind of jigsaw of different-coloured veneers. Decorative woods are cut into thin layers and made up into a pattern on the veneer sheet, which is then applied to a door panel, table top, or drawer front. Marquetry is sometimes confused with inlay, in which each individual piece forming the pattern is inserted separately into the timber.

In 1685 an event of historic importance in France had an unexpected effect upon furniture-making in England. The revocation of the Edict of Nantes by Louis XIV took away from

---

[1] In 1684 the first public library in London was established by the Rector of St-Martin-in-the-Fields, later Archbishop Tenison of Canterbury. Evelyn wrote in his diary: 'Dr Tenison communicated to me his intention of erecting a library in St Martin's Parish, for the public use, and desired my assistance, with Sir Christopher Wren, about the placing and structure thereof, a worthy and laudable design.

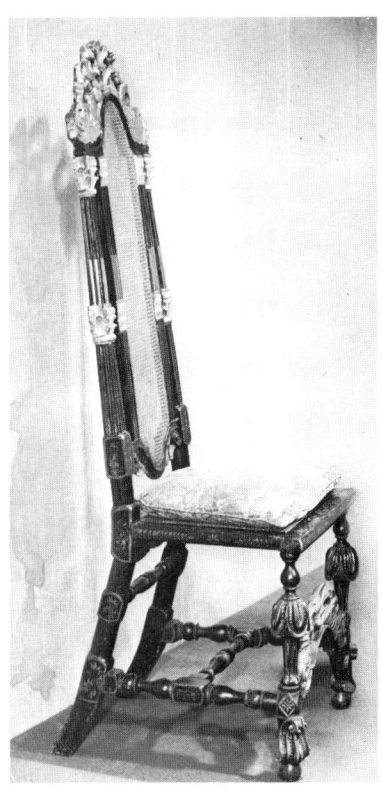

29 Elaborately carved Charles II walnut and cane chair *(left)* and *(right)* contrasted with a chair of the time of William and Mary

the Huguenots many special privileges which they had enjoyed, and the persecution which followed drove many of them to seek refuge in England. These refugees included some of the best furniture-workers in France and their influence greatly helped English craftsmen.

The most elaborate of all forms of marquetry was made by a French craftsman, André-Charles Boulle, master cabinet-maker to the Crown. His technique was to glue together a thin sheet of brass and another of mother-of-pearl or tortoiseshell and to trace a pattern on one of them. When the pattern was cut out and the sheets separated, the tortoiseshell portion was inserted into the metal ground, and vice versa. The result was two panels of elaborate marquetry, identical in design but the inverse of one another, which were usually used side by side on the same piece. Work of this kind was called 'boulle', 'boule', or 'buhl'.

There was a great increase in trade with the Far East during the seventeenth century. The Dutch and English East India Companies were bringing to Europe Oriental products of all kinds, which were at first bought as 'curiosities' rather than as pieces to use. Portugal, too, had had very close ties with the Orient since Portuguese sailors had landed in China in 1515, and when Charles II married the Portuguese princess, Catherine of Braganza, it was inevitable that Portuguese styles should begin to be fashionable in England. Among the many items of furniture which Catherine brought to England in her dowry were lacquered or 'japanned' cabinets.

Lacquering consists of treating the surfaces of wood with many coatings of sap from the lacquer tree. Each coat has to be rubbed down to make a perfectly smooth surface, before the groundwork is ready for decorating with paint and varnish.

30 An early eighteenth-century lacquer cabinet

So popular did lacquer furniture become during the late seventeenth century that English and Dutch merchants exported carcases of desks, bureaux, cabinets, and tables to the Orient to be lacquered and reshipped to Europe.

Do-It-Yourself lacquering became popular and a *Treatise on Japanning and Varnishing* was published, to help amateurs and craftsmen to make good imitations of Oriental pieces. In 1683, ten-year-old Mary Verney's father wrote to her: 'I find you have a desire to learn to Japan, as you call it, and I approve.' In 1693 an English company was formed to make and export lacquer-work and, because they thought the import of foreign lacquered furniture would be a threat to their livelihood, they persuaded parliament to impose a heavy duty on imported lacquer.

Beds

As in earlier times, the bedstead was the most important piece of furniture in a home, whether rich or poor. In well-to-do houses the beds were ornate, decorated with rich hangings, fringes, tassels, and gold braid. They still had four posts and a tester, but now the wooden parts were not carved, but were concealed by fabric, glued on to the wood. The posts were slender and were surmounted by finials, often shaped like a pineapple, an urn, or a knob, and topped with large plumes of feathers. The richer you were, the more elaborate and costly the fabrics covering your bedstead. The Puritan period temporarily checked the extravagance of fashionable taste. To indulge in luxurious display of any kind was to invite suspicion which might lead to enquiries, and many housewives of all classes must have taken down their hangings and stored away anything that was not of the plainest, in case of neighbourly gossip or prying eyes. When the glad news of the arrival of King Charles in London was heard, chests and cupboards and presses were opened, earlier finery was washed or dusted, shaken and put up again, and those who could afford it doubtless travelled to London to see what was new to buy.

Women still received their friends in their bedrooms before and after childbirth, and during times of mourning. The Countess of Salisbury 'was brought to bed of a daughter, and lyes in very richly, for the hangings of her chamber being white satin, embroidered with silver and pearl, is valued at £14,000'.

An interesting entry in Pepys's diary in 1666 indicates how general was the custom of curtaining a bed: 'I home late to Sir W. Pen's, who did give me a bed, but without curtains or hangings, all being down. So here I went the first time into a naked bed.' Perhaps Lady Pen's servants were spring-cleaning!

There was a difference between the bed coverings used in England and on the Continent, as there still is today. In 1665 Pepys wrote: 'Where though I lay the softest I ever did in my life, with a down bed after the Danish manner upon me, yet I slept very ill.' These elaborate beds, so lavishly covered with silks and velvets, had one serious disadvantage: they became easily infested with bugs and lice. We tend to forget that our ancestors, who looked so elegant and glamorous, were dirty people and lived in homes ridden with rats, fleas, and bugs. Not for another two hundred years did people begin to understand that there is a connection between dirt and disease.

Tables

Heavy oak tables with bulbous legs and solid stretchers near the floor were still used at the beginning of the century, but in newer houses, where the family ate in a dining-parlour and not in a 'hall', smaller tables were preferred. Gradually bulbous turning went out of fashion; the tendency was to thin down the turning of the legs and omit some of the carving, and bobbin-turned legs gave way to heavy barley-sugar twists after the Restoration.

Gate-legged tables, called 'falling tables', with circular, oval, or rectangular tops, were convenient and much sought after. The number of supports varied from three to twelve, oak was the most usual wood until the mid-century, but yew and fruitwoods were also popular. Later, walnut side-tables often had tops of marquetry in intricate patterns.

In the inventory of the goods and chattels of William Sabile, when he died on 23 June 1614, there is mention of a number of tables. We can only guess at their particular uses: 'one long table with a frame . . . one little square table with a cubbord . . . one table with a boxe . . . one square table'.

Until the seventeenth century, wood surfaces were either left plain or were treated with beeswax and turpentine, but by the end of the century spirit varnish was being used by London

31 A lady at her toilet. Notice the bed, the padded chairs, and the 'borde carpet'

craftsmen, though country people kept to traditional methods.

In *Sylvia* John Evelyn mentions, in 1664, the use of linseed-oil and appears to use the words 'polish' and 'varnish' interchangeably. Celia Fiennes records, on her visit to Hampton Court Palace, that she saw in a 'Large Antyroome' several 'Marble Tables in ye Peeres between the windows; white damaske window curtaines and caine chaires.'

Clocks

A capacity for mechanical invention was gradually showing itself among craftsmen all over the country. John Evelyn recorded many examples of the exceptional skill of locksmiths and other metal-workers in country districts, and this gift began to show itself in clock-making. By the end of the seventeenth century the great age of English clock-makers had begun.

Many small bracket clocks were decorated in marquetry or lacquer, with delicate brass- or silver-work incorporated in them. They only had an hour hand, the minute hand was a later refinement. Most clock-makers were blacksmiths, because English clocks were large and made of iron, for use on the outside of buildings. Clock-makers belonged, in fact, to the Blacksmiths' Company until the Clockmakers' Company was founded in 1631.

Spring clocks were known on the Continent, but were too delicate for blacksmiths to make, so wealthy Englishmen imported clocks from abroad, and continental craftsmen set up in business in England.

In 1659 there appeared an advertisement for a pendulum clock: 'clocks that go exact and keep equaller time than any now made without this regulator', and we are reminded how erratic and unpunctual life must have been until then. Thomas Bruce was, in 1685, in attendance upon Charles II on the night before the King was taken fatally ill. In his memoirs he wrote that:

> Several circumstances made the lodging very uneasy . . . a dozen dogs that came to our bed, and several pendulums that struck at the half quarter, and all not going alike, it was a continual chiming. The King constantly being used to it, it was habitual, I sleeping but indifferently. . . .

The pendulum clock had heavy weights and it was not safe to hang it on a wall. So a wooden case was made to enclose the clock, the weights, and the pendulum. It was known as the 'long-case' clock and had a glass hood covering the dial which, by now, often had two hands. The clocks were usually flat at the top, with twist columns fitted at the corners; in many of them a piece of round or oval bottle-glass was put in the large door in the front, so that the movement of the pendulum could be seen. These long-case clocks were made of oak in country districts; in wealthy homes cases of marquetry and lacquer were preferred and hoods were topped with cresting, moulding, or a pediment.

Many writers commented on the new wealth, the new luxuries which abounded. Fabian Philipps wrote in 1664:

> The people are 10 or 20 times richer in moveable and household

furniture than ever their forefathers were, every man of £10 or £20 land per annum, now having one, if not many pieces of plate in his house. Many alehouse keeper [have] a piece of plate, instead of black pots; every artisan a piece or more of plate; and others almost all their table-service in silver-plate, their dining rooms and lodging chambers richly hung with tapestry, too many of their wives hung with pearl necklaces, diamond lockets, and the most costly sorte of jewels and little tablets of the husbands pictures richly enamelled or set in gold to hang at the outside of their hearts. And some of the retailing part of them think they come too far behind their betters if they have not a kind of carpet to spread within their apartments, or shall not be enough talked of or looked upon if they had not an Indian boot-boy with a collar of silver about his neck to attend them.

But this was a period of enormous contrasts, and we may be sure that, even at the end of the century, there were thousands who were living in terrible poverty, like the weaver of Hastings with whom John Taylor, the poet, found lodging in 1623:

> No meat, no drink, no lodging (but the floor)
> No stool to sit, no lock upon the door,
> No straw to make us litter in the night,
> Nor any candlestick to hold the light.

32 An embroidered picture of a party in about 1640, which shows a covered table and a simple stool, as well as cutlery and something of the costume of the time

5 The Eighteenth Century

THE EIGHTEENTH CENTURY in England was a time of great, but unspectacular, change. Neither the people nor the Government suffered any upheaval as violent as the Reformation in the sixteenth century or the Civil War in the seventeenth. The country was at war abroad during a large part of the century, but not even the great Marlborough's victories caused such patriotic excitement as had followed Drake's defeat of the Spanish Armada.

England largely escaped the unrest prevalent in Europe at the time; the Hanoverian kings were solid, dull, men – particularly when compared with the flamboyance of Versailles – this did not matter and the ruling classes in England welcomed a sovereign who had few political ambitions. Memories of the Civil War were still painful.

This century saw England's growth from an insular agricultural kingdom to a great mercantile nation. Colonial trade became very important, making the country less dependent on Europe. The conquest of Canada and India opened the way to large accumulations of personal wealth, although the loss of the American colonies was a temporary setback to trade. The foundation of the Bank of England was a bulwark against upheaval and a great help to credit.

The middle-class Englishman was becoming important in the affairs of the new empire. It was he who mainly financed England's wars, who developed her trade, who helped her industrial growth, and who led the humanitarian movements which sprang up after the middle of the century. He began to assert himself in politics too and the long-standing social barriers between hereditary landowners and the wealthy middle class were rapidly disappearing. To marry your son or daughter to 'trade' began to have substantial advantages.

People were tolerant of change as never before; the religious and political conflicts of the sixteenth and seventeenth centuries had broadened men's minds, and the strict regulation of industry by medieval Guilds had completely broken down.

Towns were spreading, but on the whole they remained small and still provided a market for near-by rural areas. Most

33 *Mrs Congreve and her Daughters* by Reinagle *c.* 1770. The furniture is of an earlier style than the costume

people still lived in the country; the typical Englishman was the yeoman-in-the-field, not yet the man-in-the-street. By the end of the century the first Industrial Revolution was in full swing, with its speed and dirt and disregard of the worker as a person.

There was now more understanding of minority views, and men like John Wesley and George Whitefield, excluded from the churches, made a great impression with their open-air sermons; their many converts led to the establishment of new, popular, 'non-conforming' Churches, in addition to the older Presbyterians and Quakers.

The English landscape altered a great deal during this century, as natural features were 'improved' on gentlemen's estates, trees planted, and lakes dug. It was still not easy to move from one part of the country to another, for many roads were nothing more than tracks, indicating the way to go rather than making it practicable; they were quite unfit to bear the new business of the country. As the century advanced, however, and the Turnpike Acts forced the users of roads to pay tolls for their upkeep, travelling conditions improved in some areas and coach travel became comparatively fast and comfortable. Arthur Young, who travelled widely towards the end of the century, however, had some harsh things to say about Lancashire roads: 'Let me most seriously caution all travellers who may accidentally purpose to travel this horrible country, to avoid it as they would the devil; for a thousand to one but they break their necks.' It is not surprising that northerners preferred to send their goods by river and sea. However, dangerous medieval stretches of wild country and waste land were giving place to neat, enclosed, fields and pastures, fit for the new methods of farming with which many imaginative landowners were experimenting. The deepening of rivers and the building of canals also changed the face of England and opened the way to industrial development.

Leadership in politics and in taste was still largely in the hands of the nobility and of the country gentry. To them is due the mixture of elegance and crudeness, of refinement and extreme brutality, which gave the life of the time its paradoxical character.

Building

Wealthy people were wanting to spend lavishly on new houses which would demonstrate their social status. At the beginning of the century the accepted style of building was much influenced by Sir Christopher Wren. The many pleasant houses built in town and country were usually of red brick, square in plan, with a classic door, sash-windows, and a central pediment.

In the reign of George I many architects came to the fore who ignored Wren and followed the ideas of Inigo Jones. In their eyes, everything had to follow the theories of the Italian sixteenth-century architect Palladio, so the style is called Palladian. The chief patron of this style in England was Lord Burlington, whose villa at Chiswick was the most beautiful and ambitious of many large houses of the time. Most of the smaller houses in London, Bath, and other provincial towns had a central door framed with pillars and a pediment, and a parapet along the front which gave a finish to the coping above the top storey and concealed the roof and the attic windows. Whole streets, squares, and crescents had regularly placed windows, and stone bands unifying the stucco façades at the level of each floor. Stucco was all the rage; as one writer expressed it: 'No public edifice ought to be built of brick unless it is afterwards stuccoed, for a mere brick face makes a mean appearance.'

But fashion was as fickle then as now, and in the 1600s and 1700s nobody could any longer abide Palladian architecture; revivals of Greek styles were 'in' and the fashionable architects were the brothers Adam. Their most magnificent work was at Harewood House, Osterley, and Syon House; they employed Angelica Kauffmann, the celebrated painter, to decorate the ceilings, and 'Capability' Brown to landscape the gardens of these mansions, but they also designed innumerable lesser houses in many parts of the country. They were not only admirable planners, designers, and decorators, they were also expert publicists and writers. Because of this, their style became very quickly known and influenced village masons, carpenters, and other craftsmen all over the country.

Rooms

A man of taste in eighteenth-century England lived in surroundings which have never been surpassed for elegance and fine craftsmanship. This was an age when the smallest trifle – an ornamental buckle, a lock, an embroidered waistcoat – achieved beauty and refinement.

Inside the house symmetry was as important as it was in the design of streets and house fronts. In 1785 J. MacPacke commented:

> . . . for my part, I would as soon forgive a sculptor, who should produce a statue with a wry mouth, or with one of the eyes an inch further from the nose than the other, as an architect who should neglect the regular distribution of the several parts of his design . . . as well in the interior as exterior parts.

How little would he understand what many of our present-day sculptors are trying to say!

The dimensions of the rooms in fashionable houses were based upon the cube and the double cube, and architects used mathematical formulae to decide the 'right' sizes for doorways, windows, and fireplaces. Libraries, music-rooms, boudoirs,

34 *Saying Grace* by Joseph van Aken. Notice the chairs, the pewter dishes, and the good clothes. Evidently these are servants in a large house

studies, and withdrawing-rooms had taken the place of the long gallery of former times. The great hall was no longer a living-room, but was used for concerts and for grand social occasions. One reason why town-houses still had imposing entrance halls was in order that sedan-chairs could be stored there. The hall was the 'garage'!

Large eighteenth-century houses must have been extremely uncomfortable to live in. One lady, visiting a fine house, newly built, wrote to a friend saying that: 'the apartments are so vastly spacious that one generally sees Sir John, towards the winter, put on his hat to go from one room to another'.

And Alexander Pope expressed a similar view when he visited Blenheim Palace, built for the Duke of Marlborough:

74

> 'Tis very fine,
> But where do you sleep, where do you dine?
> I see from all ye have been telling
> That 'tis a house and not a dwelling.

Of course most people did not live in houses as grand as this. Local builders still used local materials to build on traditional lines; some families, as always happens, had their home altered to give it the new look; most people still lived in country cottages so ill-equipped, dark, and cold as to make nonsense of any sentimental view of rural living.

The 'offices' of a Georgian house usually consisted of kitchen, pantries, china-closets, wash-house, and brewery. In larger houses there was a still-room and buttery, a dairy, and a servants' hall; only a few very large houses had a 'washroom' and none had water-closets until the end of the century. The kitchens were kept as far away from the living quarters as possible and were often in a separate building connected with the main house by covered passages, so food must always have been served half-cold.

Furniture styles followed those of architecture, as always happens: when Palladian buildings were admired, furniture was simple and symmetrical in design; in the middle years of the century fashion was derived from France and furniture was elaborately decorated; later, Chinese and Gothic motifs were the rage; at the end of the century Grecian influence was all-important. Mahogany replaced walnut after about 1720.

Mahogany had been known in England for a long time, but little of it had been available until, in 1721, the Government passed an Act abolishing the heavy duty on timbers imported from any English plantation or colony. The purpose of the Act was to help the shipbuilding trade, but cabinet-makers of course took advantage of the opportunity to launch a new fashion. This reference in *The Weekly Journal or British Gazette* of 11 December 1725 indicates a regular trade in mahogany from Jamaica:

> On the 4th of this Instant at Night, the Levant Gallery, Capt. Dumaresy, bound from Jamaica to London, was lost about four Miles from Biddiford: We hear three Men were missing, but the Captain and the rest got ashore: and some mahogany Planks were saved.

A news story in *The Daily Journal* of 26 May 1726, shows that mahogany was used for a variety of purposes:

> His Majesty's Ship, the Mermaid, which is coming from Jamaica, hath on board from thence 600 Planks of the famous Mahogany or Redwood, which grows in no part of the World but the West-Indies, which Wood is to be employed in making all the inner Doors in the new Admiralty-Office now building at Whitehall; and to be used in Tables and other purposes for the said Office. The Adventure and Faulkland, which are expected home from Jamaica, are also to bring certain Quantities of the said Wood for His Majesty's Service, there being 7000 Planks contracted for at Jamaica, by His Majesty's Order, which is to be brought home from Time to Time, by the Men of War as come from thence, Duty free.

Jamaican mahogany was shipped mainly to London and the western ports of England – Bristol and Liverpool – so it must have been cabinet-makers in those counties who first used the wood for their furniture. There was not enough demand, at first, to make it worth while sending timber elsewhere either by sail or by road wagon. Most furniture was still made locally because communications were so poor. Country craftsmen used native woods, such as oak, elm, ash, and beech, but in 1747 a London timber-merchant's stock included many foreign timbers:

> He is furnished with deal from Norway, with oak from Sweden, with mahogany from Jamaica, with walnut-tree from Spain, and yellow deal from the Baltic.

At first walnut and mahogany were equally fashionable, but the newer wood gradually supplanted the older. Mahogany has a beautiful patina, great strength, and a good resistance to worm. It has a wide range of colour and figuring and can be cut into very wide boards. This fact had an influence upon the breadth of table tops, cabinet doors, and bookshelves, and contributed to the broad, generous proportions of mid-eighteenth-century pieces. The use of mahogany is a good example of how material affects design.

35 A Chippendale chair of mahogany, with ribband back and richly carved knees and feet

Seating

Until the eighteenth century nearly all seating had been rectilinear – adapted, as we have seen, from the medieval box-chair; any carving on the surface had not altered the outlines. Now curves became a normal part of the design; the walnut chair of the period has its back curved in outline, there is a curve to fit the shape of the body, the splat is curved and the space on either side of it forms a flowing curve, the seat is curved, the front and back legs are curved, and there is curved carving on the feet.

The front legs of this chair are 'cabriole' legs, curved outwards at the knee and inwards at the foot – a shape which was new at the beginning of the eighteenth century and remained in fashion for the next fifty years. For the first time, furniture-makers were confident enough to make chairs without stretchers, which had previously been needed to brace the legs.

Elegant cabriole legs needed elegant feet and these were

shaped like horses' hooves, lions' paws, or birds' claws. The most fashionable of all were 'ball and claw' feet, a design representing a dragon's claw holding a pearl, which had been used in the East since the third century A.D. The ball and claw foot added to the cost of a set of chairs, not only in the carving, but also in the material, and a number of the cheaper sets of chairs had turned bun feet instead. Chair knees were sometimes carved with masks, leaves, or shells, and the arms finished with eagles' heads.

All these curves and a certain elegant cosiness which is characteristic of much of the walnut furniture of the early eighteenth century, gave way to a more rectangular look when mahogany became fashionable. Walnut pieces began to seem old-fashioned and were, in many families, stored away in attics and stables.

The year the chair on page 77 was made (1754) was also the date of the publication of Thomas Chippendale's *Gentleman and Cabinet-Maker's Director*. The word 'gentleman' in the title reminds us that this was the age of the wealthy man of taste and the cultured patron of the arts. Within seven years the *Director* had been issued in three editions; the list of subscribers shows that they were, as the author said, 'patrons and customers in all classes of society' and not only the very rich. There was no need for Chippendale to issue a trade card, for the *Director* and other books of designs issued by him and his son spread their fame far and wide.

The typical Chippendale chair was made of mahogany and the splat was a particularly important feature, with intricate piercing or delicate carving. These chairs had elegance and, for the first time, real comfort too.

William Whitehead, Poet Laureate, wrote an article on *Taste* in 1753, in which he recorded:

> ... a few years ago everything was Gothic; our houses, our beds, our bookcases, our couches ... according to the present prevailing whim, everything is Chinese, or in the Chinese taste ... chairs, tables, frames for looking glasses are all reduced to this new-fangled standard.

Chinese chairs, with their fretted backs, were not strong. Chippendale thought them undesirable for use in the dining-room, but 'very proper for a Lady's Dressing-Room; especially if it is hung with India Paper'. (Chinese wallpaper was the height of fashion, but was called 'Indian' probably because it was brought to England by the East India Company.)

Thomas Chippendale was not responsible for all the designs issued under his name, for he employed 'ghosts' to help him. He was a designer, and a keen businessman; he travelled about the country a great deal to attend to customers and to discuss their requirements, and he could not have had time to see personally to all the work being done in his workshop. Credit for the quality of the workmanship of eighteenth-century furniture is due to the foremen of the workshops and to the workmen themselves, all of whom are unknown.

Emigrants to the New World took with them what furniture they could and some pieces belonging to the wealthier families had been made in Chippendale's workshops. Imported luxuries were always in demand by the Settlers and a traveller to New England in 1741 reported

> ... that a Gentleman from London would almost think himself at home in Boston, where he observes that Number of People, their Houses, their Furniture, their Tables, their Dress and Conversation, which perhaps is as splendid and showy, as that of the most considerable Tradesmen in London.

After the middle of the century, imports from England declined as cabinet-makers in the Colony became more active and war clouds gathered. Pattern books, including the *Director* were taken across the Atlantic, and there were skilled cabinet-makers among the colonial Settlers who could make excellent copies of Chippendale's designs. One of these was Jonathan Gostelowe of Philadelphia who, himself, published a *Journeyman's Philadelphia Book of Prices* in 1795. The photograph on the page overleaf shows English furniture of 1710–60, which was taken to Virginia by colonial Governors, and remained there.

The half-century after 1760 was a particularly splendid period in English furniture-making. In 1788 Hepplewhite wrote: 'English taste and workmanship have of late years been much sought for by surrounding nations.' Hundreds of cabinet-makers, chair-makers, carvers, and gilders worked in London at that time; 2,500 are listed by Sir Ambrose Heal in *The London Furniture Makers 1660–1840*.

36 The Supper Room of the Governor's Palace, Williamsburg, Virginia. Note especially the Chinese wallpaper, the china cabinet, and two styles of mahogany chair

Robert Adam designed chairs in a delicate Greek style, with tapered legs and the backs delicately carved with plumes of feathers. This is a historic decoration in England: ever since Edward the Black Prince won his insignia of three ostrich plumes and his motto *Ich Dien* at the Battle of Crécy in 1346, every Prince of Wales has borne this badge. Between 1785 and 1800, when the future George IV, as Prince of Wales, was the leader of fashion, the feathers motif was particularly fashionable, and furniture-designers used it in various ways.

The fashionable cabinet-makers did not disdain the work of country craftsmen and these, in turn, were much influenced by London designers. This cross-fertilisation of town and country was a peculiarity of England at that time. In France, where taste was dominated by the court at Versailles, noblemen took little or no interest in their country properties; there was little contact between town and country styles and virtually no influence of the one upon the other. Furniture-making there was a luxury trade, in England it was not.

In the years of the dull, stolid, Hanoverian courts of George I and George II, English gentlemen liked to spend a large proportion of their time on their estates; they played a part in local life, and often employed local craftsmen. Their fashionable tastes had a stimulating influence upon local work.

Provincial life at the time was thriving too. For example, Joseph Wright, the great painter of the latter part of the century, was proud to be known as 'Wright of Derby', and to choose his subjects from the new Midland industrial scene; William Cobbett referred to London as 'The Great Wen'; Literary, Artistic, and Philosophical Societies in provincial towns were patronised by landed gentry, local professional men, and the 'new' men who were directing the new industries. This social mixture had a profound influence upon English life, then and later.

Conditions of furniture-making varied of course between town and country. In London, craft work was highly specialised; an anonymous writer of 1747 tells us

> Many shops in London are so richly set out that they look more like Palaces and their Stocks are of exceeding great Value. But this Business seems to consist, as do many others, of two Branches, the Maker and the Vendor; for the Shopkeeper does not always make every sort of Goods that he deals in, though he bears away the Title.

In the country the situation was quite different. In 1776 Adam Smith wrote about the varied work done by one man in a workshop: 'A country carpenter deals in every kind of work that is made of wood, he is not only a carpenter, but a joiner, a cabinet-maker and even a carver of wood.'

Another chair in use was the eighteenth-century countryman's chair, the Windsor, though these were also in use in lesser rooms of grand houses. The name 'Windsor' is given to all chairs with a solid wooden seat which has legs and parts of the back separately dowelled into it. They were first made in the Chilterns, on pole lathes set up in the beechwoods, by 'bodgers' who turned the spindles which gave the chairs their characteristic 'stick' backs.

During this period 'coaching' was highly popular in spite of bad roads, footpads, and highwaymen. It is likely that the idea for a new decoration on seating originated in an attempt to make travelling more comfortable. This was 'buttoning', called 'quilting' by coachbuilders, who used it for the inside lining of sedan-chairs as well as of coaches. Stitches of strong thread were pulled through the chair padding and fixed to the outer covering through buttons arranged in diagonal rows. This way of decorating upholstery became very popular in the nineteenth century and is sometimes still used in a lighter form.

Tables

At the beginning of the century, joiners were using wainscot oak for dining-tables, because good-quality walnut – 'the best French Wallnut tree' – was too expensive. Dining-tables were still usually gate-legged, and the two hinged leaves of the top needed a strong, straight-grained wood which would not warp. When the joiners learned about mahogany their interest was immediate, for here was a timber which could be bought in very wide planks. When they began to work with it, they found it was the perfect material for table tops: the wide planks enabled them to make each of the leaves in one piece, and the hard texture gave a perfect surface which took on a fine polish. A new type of table, with a central pillar, tripod base, and circular top, could now be made. This became so popular that most homes had at least one, and it was also used a great deal in coffee-houses and other public places. Because the carved tripod often had the legs ending in claw and ball feet,

37 The dining-room at Saltram: the ceiling, carpet, and furniture were designed by Robert Adam

such tables were often called 'claw tables' or 'pillar and claw tables'.

The great variety of tables made during this period shows us how much people's horizons were widening. Chippendale's *Director* showed designs for the following: two china-tables, two breakfast-tables, one shaving-table, seven sideboard-tables, four 'Buroe Dressing Tables', twelve commode-tables, five writing-tables, eleven library-tables, and three toilet- or dressing-tables. Many of these must have been interchangeable, some were doubtless bought only as status symbols, but nevertheless they show us how varied life was becoming for those who could afford to buy.

For large entrance halls and reception-rooms, elegant side-tables were made in pairs or in sets of four. These were intended to stand against a wall, usually between windows and with mirrors above them. The tops were often of marble, the legs at first almost straight, with club feet, and richly carved and gilded; later examples had cabriole legs and ball and claw feet, often with knees carved with a shell. These were sometimes called 'marble tables' as in this letter dated 1744 written by a Mrs Delaney:

> Yesterday my upholsterer came and my new apartment will be very handsome. The drawing room hung with tapestry, on each side of the door a Japan chest, the curtains and the chairs crimson mohair, between the windows large glasses with gilt frames, and under them marble tables with gilt stands.

One kind of side-table, called a 'console', was introduced to

38 The design on this plate shows a dressing-table, a clock, and (on the rim) a pedestal table

84

this country from France; it had only two legs at the front, and the back was screwed to the wall.

By the 1780s, many side-tables were made of satinwood, they often had semicircular tops inlaid with floral marquetry. These 'pier' tables were also intended to stand between the windows and under a mirror. Sometimes they were made in pairs so that they formed a circular table when placed together.

Dining-tables were long and generally made in sections, so that the size could be adjusted to suit the particular occasion. Some had a double-gate arrangement; others had end-sections which could be attached by hinges or clipped into brass sockets. As they were covered with a white cloth when in use, they were not usually as elaborately decorated as side-tables. At the end of the century sectional dining-tables were made with pedestal legs, so that a long table was really a number of smaller ones standing closely together.

Many of the industrial developments of the last part of the eighteenth century had an effect upon the equipment for the dining-table. The most important of these was the expansion of the pottery industry, largely due to Josiah Wedgwood, as a result of which thousands of families were, for the first time, able to eat off excellent china. Another amenity which came within the reach of the growing middle class at this time was the result of Thomas Bolsover's experiments in fusing silver on to copper. Plated tableware, looking like solid silver, but selling for about a third of the price, obviously completed the appearance of the elegant dining-table and enabled many a modest family to climb up in the social scale.

Tea-drinking was fashionable and there were tea-gardens where ordinary people could walk about or sit drinking tea, as well as more famous gardens in London, such as Ranelagh, Marylebone, and Vauxhall, where elegant people gathered to gossip and show off their clothes. Some of these tea-gardens had mineral springs where visitors could drink the waters and enjoy concerts and fireworks. Sophie von der Roche, a German who visited London, wrote in her diary in 1786 of a visit to Sadler's Wells Gardens:

> ... lakes with trees in front of the house itself, numerous avenues with delightful tables and benches for visitors, under trees hung with tiny lamps. In the open temple lower-class lasses, sailors and other young people were dancing. ...

As tea-gardens became more crowded and rowdy, people of fashion began to drink tea at home. Special pots and cups were used, each person having his own little tea-set; as early as 1707 a silver teapot had been bought by the Duke of Bedford as a special present for the Duchess.

Cabinet-makers made small 'china-tables' for domestic use. One type had an oblong top mounted on delicate cabriole legs or on straight pierced legs 'in the Chinese taste'; the other had a round top on a tripod base. There was a pierced gallery round the edge, or a scalloped 'pie-crust' edge, to protect the fragile tea-things made of precious 'china' ware. The top of a tea-table was usually hinged, so that it could stand against a wall when not in use. Tea cost as much as 45s a pound at this time, so it was wise to keep it under lock and key in a 'caddy'. The word 'caddy' is derived from *kati*, an Eastern measure of weight. At first they were called 'tea-chests' and usually matched the furniture in the room. Often they were divided into two compartments, for holding black and green tea-leaves; the inside was lined with lead foil.

Not even gin-drinking caused as much controversy as tea. Tea was heavily taxed and a great deal was smuggled into the country; so much was drunk that some families were said to have ruined themselves by it. Dorothy Wordsworth, in her Journal, records the case of a man and wife with one child who had once had 'a clear estate', but who lost it all because 'the Wife would make tea four to five times in a day'. The poor made their tea from used tea-leaves which were sold for a penny or two at the back doors of well-to-do houses. These were always the cook's 'perks'.

In the *Housekeeping Book* of Susanna Whatman, published in the middle of the century, there are interesting details about the care of furniture. Mrs Whatman, whose husband was a wealthy paper-manufacturer, originator of the 'whatman' art paper which is still used, wrote out instructions for her housekeeper and servants:

> The first thing a housekeeper should teach her new servant is to carry her candle upright. . . . One of the most useful directions next to carrying a candle upright is that of putting away chairs, tables, and anything that goes next to a wall, with the hand behind it. For want of this trifling attention, great pieces are frequently

knocked out of the stucco and the backs of the chairs, if bending, sloping backwards, leave a mark on the wall.

39 Taking tea in 1725. The different ways of holding tea-cups can be seen, and the man wears a turban in place of his wig

And for her housemaids Mrs Whatman wrote: 'The books in the library are not to be meddled with, but they may be dusted as far as the wing of a goose will get.'

John Trusler, in a book *Domestic Management* written at the end of the eighteenth century cautioned his readers about the possible carelessness of their housemaids towards the furniture:

I have seen a strong country wench, from a conception that hard rubbing is necessary, raise a cabriole chair on one leg and, in order to rub the opposite leg, lean on it with that force as to make the whole frame crack, and rub a slight table till it has given way under her heavy hand.

Card-playing for money was a passionate pastime for high society in Georgian times and many fine card-tables were made. *The Daily Courant* on 15 November 1723, advertised:

> TO BE SOLD BY THE MAKER
> At the Looking-Glass and Cabinet Ware-house . . . all sorts of Looking-Glasses and Cabinet Work, both Walnut-Tree and Japann'd; and all Sorts of Tables, as Writing Tables, Wist-Tables, Ombre-Tables. . . .

Some card-tables had cabriole legs, later ones had narrow tapered legs; the corners were usually rounded and 'dished' to hold candle-sticks, and had an extra well for money and counters. Some served the needs of both backgammon and draughts players by having double tops marked out with appropriate inlay. Some had separate candle-brackets, some were baize-covered, many had folding tops and a swing leg which was hinged to the back framework.

Pembroke tables which, according to Sheraton, derived their name from that of 'the lady who first gave orders for one of them and who gave the first idea of such a table to a workman', were also called 'breakfast-tables' and became popular after 1770. They were small, made of mahogany or satinwood, a light, yellow, fine-figured wood imported from the West Indies. They had rectangular or oval tops with two hinged side flaps, delicate tapered legs, and usually a drawer on one side. By the end of the century no fashionable room could be without one.

Sofa-tables were similar to Pembroke tables, but larger. They were intended for ladies to draw, write, or read upon.

A collection of books was now the ambition of anyone with any pretensions to culture and in many houses a room was made into a library. Library-tables had circular tops and were designed to stand in the centre or in a bay of a room. They were large and solid, often supported on a pedestal, and had drawers under the top.

A description of the activities of a typical day, given by Oliver Goldsmith in *The Vicar of Wakefield* suggests that women were not great users of the library:

> We were generally awakened in the morning by music, and on fine days rode a-hunting. The hours between breakfast and dinner the ladies devoted to dress and study; they usually read a page, and then gazed at themselves in the glass. . . . At dinner my wife took the lead; for, as she always insisted on carving everything herself, it being her mother's way, she gave us, upon these occasions, the history of every dish. When we had dined, to prevent the ladies leaving us, I generally ordered the table to be removed; and sometimes, with the music master's assistance, the girls would give us a very agreeable concert. Walking out, drinking tea, country dances, and forfeits, shortened the rest of the day, without the

40 A conversation piece by Benjamin Wilson, 1769. The chair has a loose cover of checked linen; the sewing-table probably has a lift-up top and only one drawer

assistance of cards, as I hated all manner of gaming except backgammon, at which my old friend and I sometimes took a twopenny hit.

'Dressing'-tables were small and often draped. This letter, written by Robert Adam to the Duke of Atholl in Scotland in 1768 shows how complicated the arrangement of a dressing- or 'toilet'-table could be, and what great attention was paid to detail in the equipping of a grand house.

> The Toilet Table is mark'd rather too narrow as the dressing room is scarce broad enough – the petticoat be some brocaded silk or crimson silk damask fringed at Bottom, the Top covr'd with Marseils[1] or other fine Quilting made to the shape. The shade and outside petticoat is generally the finest sheer muslin, striped, or wrought and edged with flounced or puckered lace in which they mix narrow and broad Ribbons according to the fancy of the owner or performer. The Scarf over the glass should be twice as long as the length from the Top of the Glass as it Stands in its place from the Table to the ground and half a yard more and when the Scarf is doubled the middle half yard makes the hood....

Such tables had elegant accessories, in particular little ivory or metal 'scratchers' for use when heads were irritating too much.

Although most country people probably had their furniture made locally, there was a surprising amount of trade carried on between different districts, in spite of the very bad condition of the roads. Parson Woodforde wrote in his diary in April 1789:

> About 2 o'c this afternoon two Men of Sudbury's at Norwich came with my Side-Board and a large New Mahogany Table, bought of Sudbury, brought on the men's shoulders all the way and very safe.

And earlier, in 1726, Daniel Defoe wrote in *The Compleat English Tradesman*:

> ... it is scarce credible to how many counties of England, and how remote, the furniture of but a mean house must send them ... the chairs, if of cane, are made at London; the ordinary matted chairs, perhaps in the place where they live ... tables, chests of drawers made at London; as also looking glass.

---

[1] Probably silk imported from Marseilles.

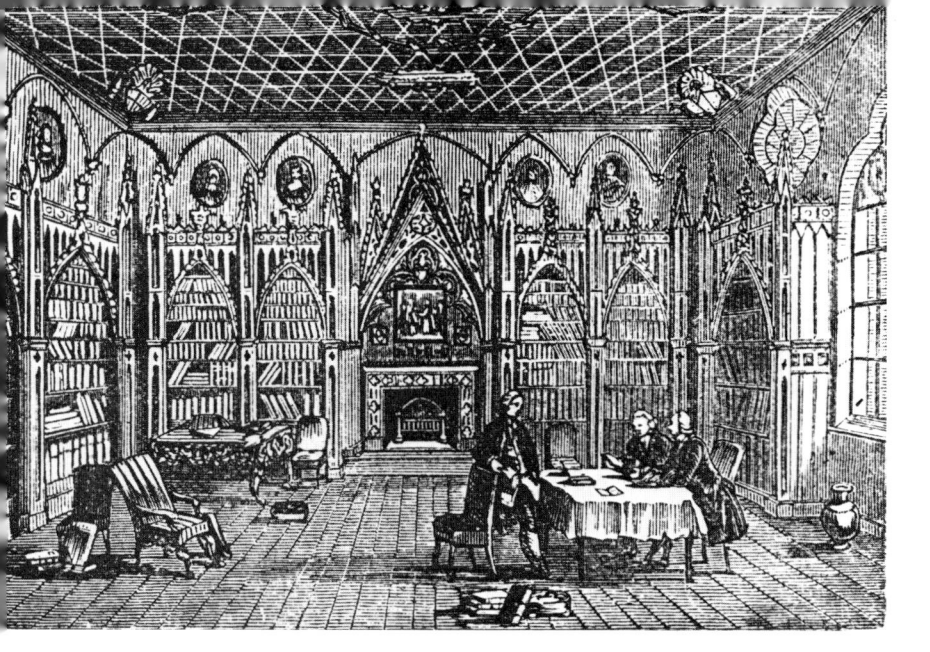

41 The library at Strawberry Hill, in the 'gothick manner'

Packing furniture for transport to distant parts of the country was a hazardous business. In 1720 a cabinet-maker named William Pearson charged £4 10s 0d for 'six Large Deale cases, Tow paper, Cord and Battins to Packing ye 24 Chares all'. Tow paper was beaten hemp or flax; the 'battins' would have been used to secure the legs of the chairs. Extra expense was incurred if the supplier sent a skilled workman to instal furnishings. In 1718 an upholder sent an employee to 'Deliver ye Goods and to put ym in thear places'; he charged £17 for 'Seventy-four dayes worke for one man and paid for an horse going down into Yorkshire and charges to and fro upon the Road.'

A good deal of English furniture went even further afield, in ships of the Royal Navy and in those taking emigrants to the Colonies. At the National Maritime Museum, at Greenwich, we can see some of the pieces which Nelson had aboard the *Victory*, and the trade card of Thomas Butler, London cabinet-maker in 1800, tells us that he sold: 'Bed furniture and Mattresses calculated for the East and West Indies. Ship cabbins furnished. Articles particularly adapted and for Travelling and Exportation.'

42 A lady of the eighteenth century receiving guests in bed, from a picture by Moreau

Beds

The French custom of receiving guests in bed was still fashionable and bedrooms were often as finely furnished as drawing-rooms. Jonathan Swift related that he dined with a lady who was ill in bed and they were served with three herrings and a chicken.

Bedsteads were enormous throughout most of this period; they still had four posts, with a high canopy and a roof. Some were japanned in the Chinese style and James Boswell, in his *London Journal* wrote that he 'slept in a handsome tent bed with green and white check curtains. It gave a snug yet genteel look to my room.'

Celia Fiennes, visiting grand houses at the beginning of the century, described a bedroom in a house at Epsom:

> You enter one room hung with crosstitch in silks, the bed the same lined with yellow and white strip'd satin, window curtains white silk damaske, with furbellows of callicoe printed flowers, the chaires crosstitch, and two stooles of yellow mohaire with crosstitch. . . .

State beds were still very elaborate; in 1726 Lady Bute described a mourning bed:

> The apartments, the staircase, and all that could be seen of the house, were hung with black cloth; the Duchess, closely veiled with crape, sate upright in her state bed under a high black canopy, and at the foot stood, ranged like a row of servants at morning prayer, the grandchildren of the deceased Duke.

Gradually, the wooden parts of bedsteads were not so completely covered in fabric; cornice, tester, and posts were often made of carved and polished mahogany, uncovered, and towards the end of the century the posts were often gracefully fluted. Half-tester beds, with canopy and curtains at the head only, were a complete break with tradition. Couch-beds were made as divans or couches, with a wooden headboard and footboard and low wooden sides. These were often fitted with roll cushions, very like those on day-couches.

In 1740 a Mrs Purefoy, living in Buckinghamshire, sent an order to a Mr Baxter in Henrietta Street, Covent Garden, London, for

> some patterns of Quilting you mention, together with the lowest price of each Pattern. I shall want enough to make one of the new-fashioned Low Beds without a cornice, if I like the Quilting and the Price I will let you know the Quantity.

Many well-to-do country families arranged for some of their requirements to be bought for them in London, either by somebody living there whom they paid to be their agent, or by a carrier who travelled between London and the nearest provincial town. In letters written during the eighteenth century we find mention of carriers bringing furniture, fine materials for making clothes and curtains, and special foodstuffs.

At this time shopkeepers sometimes sold many other goods besides their main articles of trade. In 1730 there was a cabinet-maker named John Speer who sold women's hats, chairs, mats, and all kinds of small articles made of wood, and a Mr Wilson issued a trade card on which he described himself as 'a dealer in coles' but selling also 'chairs, organs, harpsichords and pianofortes'!

Coverings for beds were very expensive. Mattresses on good beds were stuffed with feathers – either those of swans, geese, ducks, or hens, according to your income. If you lived in the country you saved feathers whenever you could, picked them over carefully and washed them, then dried them in the bread oven after baking time. Children collected other fillings for pillows: thistledown, willow catkins, bog moss, cotton grass, and chopped straw were easily available. Straw was also plaited into palliasses to put under mattresses to preserve them. Humble people had little but palliasses to sleep on, but servants in grand households were sometimes very well accommodated. The Duke of Bedford's housekeeper had two rooms and a closet, and the kitchen-maid had a room to herself with 'a four post bed, with green hartteen, a feather bed, bolster and pillows, a rug and a lindsey bed-quilt and four blankets'.

We are reminded of the very bad road conditions, even in the later eighteenth century, by an invoice for goods supplied to Lord Hopetoun at Hopetoun House, West Lothian, by a London cabinet-maker in 1768. Robert Adam, architect, had been commissioned to enlarge Hopetoun House and James Cullen, cabinet-maker of Greek Street, Soho, travelled to Scotland with him to discuss the design of furniture and hangings for the State Apartments. When the furniture was to be dispatched, it was evidently thought that it would be safer to send it by sea from London to Scotland, for among the archives at Hopetoun House there is an

> Invoice of Goods ship'd on board the King George, Captn Marshill, belonging to the Right Honble the Earl of Hoptoun, June the 28th 1768 viz.
> No. 1   A case containing . . . all the Curtains, Vallens, Bases, 2 inside Cornices, 4 gilt vauses and all the small Ornaments and Leaves . . . a larg wrapper and a coverlet to pack the whole – all belonging to the State Bed

Item 3 A Case containing ... The carv'd and gilt feet posts of the Bed and polish'd Rod. ...

David Garrick's bed, dating from 1770, can be seen in its original condition in the Victoria and Albert Museum. It is 'in the Chinese manner', very elegant, with printed Indian cotton hangings.

Standards of hygiene were virtually non-existent, fleas and bed bugs were common, even in noble households, and seem to have been accepted with good humour. When Parson Woodforde stayed at La Belle Sauvage Inn in London in 1782, he wrote in his diary: 'A very good House it is ... I was bit terribly

43 David Garrick's bed of 1770 – in the 'Chinese manner'

by the Buggs last night, but they did not wake me.' A year or two later he stayed at the same inn and was obliged to sit up all night in a chair because he was 'very much pestered and bit by the Buggs'.

In *A Treatise of Buggs* written in 1730, J. Southall advised caution in handling furniture:

> Examine well all furniture that comes in, before you set it up, Beds especially; which I recommend should be plain, and as free from wood-work as possible, and made to draw out, that the Wainscot and Walls may be better come at, to clear them from Buggs and dirt. . . . Oak-bedsteds, and plain Wainscot Head-Boards, and Tester-Rails of that Wood, allow them the least Harbour and no Food; such therefore I recommend. . . . If for Ornament you use Lace, let it be sewed, not pasted on, for Paste they love much. . . .

A London cabinet-maker advertised an 'infallible method' of preventing bugs, though only the wealthiest of his clients would have been willing to go to the length of importing a special wood from Jamaica for the purpose:

> Young Lady Catherine Brydges had been bit in her cradle by these disrespectful creatures; but after her crib had been lined with slips of bitterwood, her ladyship had never been bit since.

In grand families a new kind of cradle was in use, hanging on posts, with panels of cane at the sides. Here is a bill for a very elaborate cradle made in the middle of the century:

> For a large State Cradle with a Canopy Top and curved Ornaments to clip each Corner and round the bottom and top and up the Front and the Head with a Crown and plume of Feathers for the Top and Lyone heads at each end of the rockers all Gilt in Burnished Gold and two pairs of neate Chased Handles . . . £52.

Storage

At a time when people's possessions are increasing, they are likely to want many varieties of furniture in which to store things. A writer towards the end of the eighteenth century referred to 'the fashion of the day, to resort to a number of contrivances for making one piece of furniture serve many

44   The magnificent State Bedroom at Osterley House, designed by Robert Adam

purposes'. One favourite feature in new rooms was an alcove or niche, built into one corner, often with a curved top and pilasters on either side. This was the earliest kind of built-in storage furniture and was generally used to display porcelain or silver.

Chests-of-drawers did not change much, except in details. In country districts tallboys were made of walnut and of mahogany. They usually had seven or more drawers, three or four in the lower part and three or four above, with a small pair immediately below the cornice. The top drawers must have been inconveniently high, but being small they could be removed from the carcase by anyone of average height. We know that these small top drawers were continually being taken out and replaced, because there are often marks on the rail below the drawers and also on the front of the drawer below.

The name 'chest' was not much used after the middle of the century, for the French name *'commode'* became fashionable and referred to any piece fitted with drawers. Some low commodes had the top drawer hinged so that it could be opened as a writing flap, many were bow-fronted or serpentine-fronted.

'Dressing buroes' were fashionable during the reigns of the first two Georges. They were narrow pieces, made in both walnut and mahogany, and of particularly fine craftsmanship. We may ask, in these days when we dress in our bedrooms and write in our sitting-rooms or studies, why our ancestors wanted a piece of furniture which combined both activities – writing and dressing. The answer to this query is given by a mid-eighteenth-century architect who was planning a mansion 'for a nobleman of the most distinguished taste, and adorned at the greatest expense'. He says:

> A dressing-room in the house of a person of fashion is a room of consequence, not only for its natural use in being the place of dressing, but for the several persons who are seen there. The morning is a time many choose for dispatching business; and as persons of this rank are not to be supposed to wait for people of that kind, they naturally give them orders to come about a certain hour, and admit them while they are dressing.

So the dressing-room of the master of the family was always on the ground floor. If interrupted by a tradesman while dressing – which in the eighteenth century took as much time for 'a person of fashion' as it does for a smart woman today – he could write a note, sign a paper, or discuss an account while powdering his wig or pomading his face.

A similar piece of furniture was the writing-bureau-on-stand, which had no dressing-glass or toilet drawer, and was used only for writing. This was convenient for small rooms, a boudoir, an ante-room, or a bedroom.

It was not only men of letters and noblemen who now had libraries; the country squire and the middle-class merchant usually had some books and needed a case in which to keep them. Even sham bookcases and bureaux which had beds inside them were a status symbol, but also had practical uses. This was an hospitable age, people visited a great deal and drank a great deal, so it was often necessary to put visitors up for the night. If the spare room were occupied it was convenient to be able to offer them even a bureau or a bookcase to sleep in!

The poor still had only a few, rough home-made pieces of furniture, and their rooms contained little but bare necessities. Oliver Goldsmith, in *The Deserted Village* (1770), wrote of the village chest which '. . . contrived a double debt to pay, A bed by night, a chest of drawers by day'.

Dressers continued as utilitarian pieces for homely living-rooms and kitchens. They were usually made by country craftsmen, who were not much influenced by changes of fashion; they were still made of oak, which suited their construction; their shape did not change, because their purpose did not change, and they had no status value.

The sideboard developed as the dining-room became a separate place for family meals. When the plate and cutlery were stored in the pantry, a side table was sufficient for serving, but gradually all kinds of small, independent pieces of furniture for dining purposes became fashionable. Wine-coolers, water-urns, plate-warming cupboards, and knife-boxes began to be grouped round the side-table.

Robert Adam was the first designer to add pedestals to the side-table and it was he who developed the idea of an all-in-one sideboard. In his *Drawing Book* of 1791, Thomas Sheraton described such a piece:

> In spacious dining-rooms the sideboards are often made without drawers of any sort, having simply a rail, a little ornament, and pedestals with vases, which produce a grand effect. One pedestal is used as a plate-warmer and is lined with tin; the other as a pot cupboard,[1] and sometimes a cellarette for wine. The vases are used for water, for the use of the butler.

The next stage in the evolution of the sideboard was the introduction of drawers with cupboards below. Gradually an all-in-one piece became fashionable which, by the next century, had become a conventional necessity, on which tea-caddy, biscuit-barrel, and perhaps an aspidistra had pride of place.

A writer of 1786 commented:

[1] To save the gentlemen the trouble of going to the privy!

A well-educated British gentleman is of no country whatever, he unites in himself the characteristics of all foreign nations; he talks and dresses in French, and sings in Italian; he rivals the Spaniard in indolence, and the German in drinking; his house is Grecian; his offices Gothic; and his furniture Chinese.

As this century of many fashions ended, English men and women began to feel a romantic wish to return to their native heritage. The high promise of the French Revolution ended in disillusionment, and twenty years of war against France afterwards caused our more stable society to withdraw into itself. But the eclecticism of the Georgian period resulted in the negation of any style, and the beginning of the chaos which was to prevail throughout the next century.

45 A library chair of the eighteenth century. The back is designed to form a book-rest or writing-table

6 *The Nineteenth Century*

THE NINETEENTH CENTURY was, throughout Europe, a period of immense and revolutionary change; England blazed the trail in the use of machinery in industry, and managed to survive the stresses involved in altering, in only a hundred years, the whole basis of national life.

For over sixty years England lived under the rule of a queen. The influence of this mother-figure did much to unify the nation and it is remarkable that the country avoided revolution, when so many continental peoples were in turmoil. The enthusiasm of the Prince Consort encouraged a new interest in the arts and sciences, and a new solemnity in human affairs. The Victorians did much to remove from daily life the brutality and coarseness which the eighteenth century had tolerated, and great efforts were made to reduce corruption in public affairs. The temper of the times was to govern, to curtail the power of the landed classes in the interests of business. There was opportunity for initiative as never before; a settled belief in the importance of individual responsibility caused unparalleled industrial and commercial development, and also an awakening of the social conscience.

A series of great reforms led gradually to improvements in housing, in prisons, in the insanitary conditions of towns, in working conditions in factories, and to an extension of the vote to the working man and a modicum of education to all children.

There was intense opposition to centralisation, but Whitehall officials gradually came to supervise and control a new network of local government, while the setting up of the County Councils in 1888 helped to improve standards of administration. The police, who were at first seen to be a threat to civil liberties, gradually earned the confidence of the public, and life became safer and less unjust than ever before.

At the beginning of the century Britain was a loose grouping of regions with marked differences in habits, in culture, in speech, and in buildings. These were gradually welded together by the powerful unifying force of the railways, and also by the penny post, the cheap national newspapers, and the electric telegraph. London had always dominated national life to a certain extent, but now for the first time other great cities became powerful and Britain was becoming a smaller, crowded country.

This was a young age; families were large and the expectation of life was still low. The Victorian virtues taught in all families, high and low, strict and less strict, were those of sobriety, thrift, piety, hard work, and obedience. These characteristics, allied to the brilliance of engineers, the initiative of merchants and administrators, and the zeal of missionaries, carried British influence and power across the world. The empire gave plentiful scope for initiative and adventure and the 'Mother' country gained in self-confidence as well as materially and spiritually.

Agriculture was prosperous in the 1870s, and contributed to the steadily improving standard of living; but the gradual development of fast refrigerated ships favoured the more competitive products from Australia and New Zealand, and British farming suffered.

Fear of rising discontent and a genuine desire to improve the conditions of the poor brought about a remarkable increase in charities during the first half of the century. Although ostentation and vanity may often have been among the original motives for this, private benevolence persisted long after the fear of revolution was removed, and continued when many of the services, formerly undertaken by charity, had become the responsibility of the State.

Religion played a large part in stabilising the people during such an explosive period. The Churches gave to all classes a creed which was made the basis of morality and, at the same time, a justification for wealth and power: each man had his proper station in life and most were content to accept it. There was a code of Sabbath observance, of philanthropy, of discipline in the home, of regularity and responsibility in affairs, which was the strongest binding force in the nation. It was called 'respectability'.

Building

This was an age of revivals in architecture, with Gothic and Classical styles as first favourites. Houses of the well-to-do were solidly built, with large bay-windows, projecting porches and pinnacles, and ornate chimney-stacks. Owing to improved transport a variety of materials was available and houses were often built of a mixture of stone, brick, terracotta, slate, and tiles. The eighteenth-century idea of a street as being a unified whole was completely out of tune with the aggressive individualism of the nineteenth century; the rich man's home was thought of as a statement of his personal achievement, to be built as distinctly as possible, with no concern for good neighbourliness.

John Ruskin, who disliked the orderly beauty of classic designs and wrote that 'ornamentation is the principal part of architecture', urged people to add Gothic features and oddments to their houses. 'Do not be afraid of incongruities', he said in his Lectures on Architecture and Painting in 1854, 'your existing houses will be none the worse for having little bits of better work fitted to them; build a porch or point a window, if you can do nothing else.' So, many a fine eighteenth-century house was spoilt by having stucco bay-windows or 'Elizabethan' gables added to it, and the new suburbs that were thrusting into the countryside displayed a similar mixture of ideas, drawn from German castles, Gothic cathedrals, French châteaux, and Italian Renaissance palaces.

At this time it was left to engineers, such as Telford and Brunel, to exploit to the full the many new materials and new techniques available, while the architects argued about the merits and the moral implications of one historic style or another. In no previous age had so much building been done. To encourage house-building for the rapidly rising population, the tax on bricks was repealed in 1850, that on windows in 1851; there was no Government control on what was built and only very rudimentary by-laws. The barbarous poverty and overcrowding of the industrial towns were caused not only by lack of care and lack of controls, but by the fact that it had become economically necessary that work-people should live near coal-producing areas. The increased population in those areas was housed by building miles of shoddy back-to-back hovels, without gardens, without proper water-supply or sanitation, and all grossly overcrowded. Only the very cheapest materials were used; inferior bricks were set in the poorest mortar and good timber was very scarce at first because of the demands of the Royal Navy during the Napoleonic Wars and, later, because of the growing demand for pit-props, millwheels, pipes and virtually everything industrial before iron and steel were adequate.

The 'romantic' years, when Constable and Turner were painting and Wordsworth, Keats, and Shelley wrote poetry of beauty, love, and innocence, were for working men and women and children years of misery and darkness. The biggest windows were in the mills, designed to let in every hour of daylight for the increasing labour which the machines and the masters demanded.

Charles Dickens was one of many people who protested about housing conditions; one of the improvements he suggested in a letter to the Baroness Burdett-Coutts, was that large blocks of houses should be built for working people:

> It is a very good thing to try several descriptions of houses, but I have no doubt myself that the large houses are best. You can never, for the same money, offer anything like the same advantages in small houses. . . . If they had been discouraged long ago, London would be an immeasurably healthier place than it can be made in scores of years to come. If you go into any common outskirts of the town now and see the advancing army of brick and mortar laying waste the country fields and shutting out the air, you cannot fail to be struck by the consideration that if large buildings had been erected for the working people, instead of the absurd and expensive walnut shells in which they live, London would be about a third of its present size, and every family would have a country walk miles nearer to their own door. . . . Besides this, men would be nearer to their work – would not have to dine at public houses – there would be thicker walls of separation than you can ever give in small tenements – and they would have gas, water, drainage, and a variety of other humanizing things which you can't give them so well in little houses.

Some consciences were aroused by the protests of Dickens and other writers and politicians, and urban housing was the subject of numerous Reports and Royal Commissions. The early 1840s saw a decided improvement in the standard of living of the working population. According to one report, working-class houses in Sheffield, for example, were 'furnished in a very comfortable manner, the floors carpeted, and the tables are usually of mahogany; chest of drawers of the same material are commonly seen, and so in most cases is a clock also . . .'. But perhaps Sheffield was a favoured area. By the

46 The drawing-room at Berkeley Castle, Gloucestershire, furnished in a mixture of styles in the 1880s

middle of the century, modern tenements were being built in one or two places and model estates round the factories of a very few imaginative industrialists. The building of the first planned estates of Bedford Park, Port Sunlight, and Bournville inaugurated a new attitude to the design of smaller houses.

The great Public Health Act 1875 gave Local Authorities power to enforce regulations about damp-proofing, sewage disposal, and drainage. Houses built after that date were a great improvement, but the layout of urban housing schemes was still standardised and ugly. Octavia Hill organised the rebuilding of slum areas, George Peabody founded a trust for providing better housing conditions, and in 1890 Local Authorities were for the first time given powers to build houses themselves.

Rooms

Regency rooms had a feeling of lightness; the windows were large and draped with white curtains, striped or delicately sprigged in pale colours; walls, too, were in striped or sprigged papers. Much of the formal grace and order of eighteenth-century rooms was now disappearing. In his *Journal of a Tour in Great Britain*, L. Simond wrote of a visit to Osterley Park in 1811;

> Tables and chairs were studiously deranged about the fire places, and in the middle of the room, as if the family had just left them . . . Such is the modern fashion of placing furniture, carried to an extreme, that the apartments of a fashionable house look like an upholsterer's or a cabinet-maker's shop.

It is perhaps surprising that French influence continued in England, in spite of the long wars with France until 1815. But the many craftsmen who took refuge here from the Revolution brought their techniques and their ideas with them, and moreover, France had been the arbiter of European taste for so long that her prestige did not disappear easily. Ackerman expressed this in 1815 in *The Repository of the Arts:*

> The interchange of feeling between this country and France, as it relates to matters of taste, has not been wholly suspended during the long and awful conflicts which have greatly abridged the intercourse of the two nations.

47 A smoking-room 'in the Oriental style' from a catalogue of 1888

There was a great revival of Chinese taste early in the century, partly due to the influence of the Prince of Wales. Carlton House, his London home, had a Chinese drawing-room; a Chinese Gallery was built on to his house at Brighton in 1802, in order to display some Chinese wallpaper which had been given to him; and between 1815 and 1820 John Nash was employed in planning the fantastic Chinese Pavilion which still stands there.

In *Our Village* which she wrote between 1824 and 1830, Mary Russell Mitford described a fashionable house:

> Every room is a masquerade: the saloon Chinese, full of jars and mandarins and pagodas; the library Egyptian, all covered with hieroglyphics, and swarming with furniture crocodiles and sphyinxes. They sleep in Turkish tents and dine in a Gothic chapel . . . the properties are apt to get shifted from one scene to another.

The comfort, formality, and vulgarity of the upper-class Victorian home seems to us remarkable. Well-to-do families were not satisfied with the simple plan of Georgian and Regency houses, but needed a number of rooms for special purposes: a drawing-room, a dining-room, a breakfast-room, a study, a library, and a smoking-room[1] on the ground floor, with bedrooms connected by corridors on the first floor. All these rooms were dark in tone, with lace curtains in addition to heavy plush ones;[2] wallpapers were darker and heavily patterned. By 1860 rooms were filled to overflowing with old and new furniture, ornaments, and knick-knacks, so there was hardly any floor space in between. No wonder children were kept out of the grown-ups' rooms, in day and night nurseries.

The principal rooms were spacious, but the servants' quarters, in attics and basements, were dark and rambling. A wealthy continental visitor wrote home describing an important English house at which he had stayed:

> The servants live in a large room in a remote part of the house, generally on the ground floor, where all, male and female, eat together, and where the bells of the whole house are placed. . . . Each of the servants has a separate bedchamber in the highest story. Only the housekeeper and the butler have distinct apartments below. Immediately adjoining that of the housekeeper is a

---

[1] Where gentlemen kept their smoking-jackets and smoking-caps, so that their clothes and hair did not smell when they were in the other rooms.
[2] In the 1840s, with the introduction of plate-glass, large panes became fashionable and glazing bars were no longer popular. So-called 'French' windows were introduced.

room where coffee is made and the storeroom containing everything required for breakfast, which important meal, in England, belongs especially to her department. . . . On the other side of this building is the washing establishment with a small courtyard attached; it consists of three rooms, the first for washing, the second for ironing, the third which is considerably loftier and heated by steam, for drying the linen in bad weather. Near the butler's room is his pantry, a spacious fire-proof room, with closets on every side for the reception of plate, which he cleans here, and the glass and china used at dinner, which must be delivered back into his custody as soon as it is washed by the women. All these arrangements are executed with the greatest punctuality. A locked staircase leads from the pantry into the beer and wine cellar, which is likewise under the butler's jurisdiction.[1]

And here is a description of a vicarage in 1850, from a letter:

There were no bath rooms then, and all hot and cold water had to be carried from the kitchen and scullery. But we all had baths each day in spite of that. Oil lamps and candles were used for lighting. Our drawing-room was papered with a buff and gilt Fleur-de-Lys patterned paper. There were book shelves and pier glasses and wool work ottomans and an upright grand piano with faded red silk, fluted across the front and a very fine harp. The harp was a popular instrument in my mother's youth. . . .[2]

During the whole of the nineteenth century, traditional crafts survived in country districts, but gradually machines were replacing hand craftsmanship and work was becoming more specialised. A 'Manufacturer' had formerly been somebody who made something by *hand*, but now he was a businessman, and the liberal philosophy of the time allowed him to produce anything, however shoddy and hideous, if he could get away with it.

It seemed incredible then that the machine could reproduce easily the work of human hands; there was widespread pride in the vast technical changes, and it is not surprising that everyone wanted novelty and ostentation in their houses. The mantels of homes both rich and modest were overloaded with innumerable china ornaments – as if proclaiming the miracle of mass-production. A style that looked rich came into fashion,

[1] Quoted in *Early Victorian England*, ed. G. M. Young.
[2] *Ibid.*

48 *A Tea Party* by Thomas Webster, 1880. The painting shows something of what the interior of a poor home was like

suited to the needs of the new rich customers who had made their money from trade and the new industries. Quality, simplicity, and restraint were not in the mood of the time. By modern standards the period was inexpressibly vulgar, but there is no more reason to apply modern standards to this period than to any other.

The wealthy landowning class whose taste had formed Georgian England were occupied for a whole generation with the wars against France. Developments at home were left largely in the hands of a new class of 'risen' men, who had great opportunities but no experience in the use of the new powers and therefore made many mistakes. However, the increasing population would have caused some of the difficulties which arose, even if manufacture had remained a hand process.

At the Great Exhibition of 1851, conceived by Prince Albert as an opportunity of showing the artistic and industrial achievements of the time, the elegance of the glass building – 'The

Crystal Palace' as it was christened by *Punch* – contrasted sharply with the mass of overdecorated rubbish which was on view.

A reaction was inevitable and during the last thirty years of the nineteenth century a group of English architects revolted against the ornate vulgarity of popular taste. Their chief inspiration came from John Ruskin, whose *Modern Painters*, published in 1843, had started an aesthetic revolt which led to the foundation of the Pre-Raphaelite Brotherhood. The members of the Brotherhood – the painters Holman Hunt, Ford Madox Brown, Sir John Millais, Dante Gabriel Rossetti, and Sir Edward Burne-Jones, among others – were reformers who strongly disapproved of the age in which they lived and set out to put it right. They preached a return to the simplicity of nature and the destruction of industrialism; they were escapists and wished for a return to medieval craftsmanship.

William Morris was one of the Brotherhood, but different: he was craftsman, poet, and artist, but also a social reformer, a man of action. He had a dynamic impact upon the intelligentsia of his time and rekindled the love of craftsmanship. His range of activity was immense; he designed wallpaper, stained glass, ironwork, embroidery, tapestry, weaving, woodcarving, lettering, and furniture; he thought and wrote and lectured on the problems produced by the machine and upon the social condition of art. He preached, 'I don't want art for a few, any more than education for a few, or freedom for a few'; yet when he pleaded for a return to handicraft, he was, inevitably, refusing to the majority of people the great benefits of cheap, mass-produced goods. He wanted, as he wrote; 'art by the people and for the people', but he had to admit that 'all art costs time, trouble and thought' and can, therefore, never be accessible for everyone to buy.

In the 1870s the new style of interior decoration was called 'art' or 'aesthetic'. These adjectives were intended to show disapproval of the vulgarity and overdecoration of current taste, and to underline the division between art and manufacture. The Aesthetic movement was a self-conscious revival of the decorative arts and had a missionary, educational flavour. One of its leaders was Oscar Wilde, who had also been much influenced by Ruskin; he was a passionate devotee of the new movement and wrote and lectured about it.

Subdued colours were the mark of an artistic, enlightened home, especially the dull greens of wallpapers by Morris and Lewis Day. An article in the *Furniture Gazette* of 1875 described the dining-room of an 'aesthetic' house:

> the walls are a dark drab, with a high dado of mauve and drab in alternate bands, and a freize of sober hued, stamped leather. A curtain . . . which is the work of the lady of the house is a quite perfect work of art. In colour it is dark, blueish green and it is crossed by broad bands of pale yellow and black velvet beneath which are embroidered circular devices of peacock feathers.

In the same year, the *Gloucester Chronicle*, describing the entries to the Bath and West Show at Worcester, wrote:

> . . . special attention will be directed to the assortment of Art Furniture designed and manufactured by Mr C. Trapnell of Bristol. . . . The following are among the departments illustrated: 1. Farmhouse and Cottage Furniture, 2. Clergy and Country Villa Furniture, 3. Superior Furniture for Country and Town Mansions. . . .

What stratification, what a caste system that implies, with everybody neatly in his place! The rich man in his castle, the poor man at his gate – not only had God made them high and lowly, but Mr Trapnell had furniture suited to their estate.
A number of periodicals devoted to home decoration were started in the 1870s; one such journal commented in 1876:

> . . . there has assuredly never been since the world began an age in which people thought, talked, wrote and spent such inordinate sums of money and hours of time in cultivating and indulging their tastes.

Furniture-makers found it prudent to add the word 'art' to their name. The *London Trades Directory* listed 'Art Furniture Manufacturers' separately from 'Cabinet-Makers', and 'Art Tile-Painters' and 'Art Metal-Workers' were among others who adopted the new appendage to their title. 'Art' and 'aesthetic' had become the adjectives to describe almost anything that was fashionable.

One effect of William Morris's teaching and of the great interest in 'art' objects was that a number of young artists and architects decided to devote their lives to the crafts. This was a

49 The South Drawing Room at the Royal Pavilion, Brighton. The elegant suite of Dolphin furniture was made in 1813 in memory of Lord Nelson

revolutionary attitude, for craftsmanship had been despised since the end of the eighteenth century. Between 1880 and 1890 a number of societies for the promotion of artistic craftsmanship were founded in England. The Artworkers' Guild was founded in 1884 under Morris's influence – the medieval-sounding name was significant of their intense interest in the status of the craftsman. The Arts and Crafts Exhibition Society held many exhibitions of handicrafts and fostered simplicity and honesty in design; the result was a revival of artistic craftsmanship, not the development of industrial art.

Seating

Regency furniture was inspired by a variety of foreign influences, French, Egyptian, Greek, and Chinese. Napoleon's campaign in Egypt had advertised that country and Nelson's victory of the Nile had brought Egyptian designs into prominence. In 1802 a French scholar, Director-General of Museums in France, published a book on Egyptian art and ornament. It was translated into English and had a strong influence upon furniture-designers. Thomas Hope warned in 1802 of 'the extravagant caricatures which have of late begun to start up in every corner of the capital'.

Archeological discoveries in Greece and Italy had attracted people's interest to Classical styles once again. Greek influence was at its height when the Parthenon sculptures were bought in England by public subscription in 1816, and, when the Greeks revolted against the Turks in 1821, English intellectuals felt immediate sympathy. This sympathetic political interest was inevitably reflected in the things made and sold.

Increasing trade with the East was attracting attention to Chinese designs, and the revival was accentuated by the influence of the Prince of Wales. Japanned furniture was decorated with pagodas, mandarins, and dragons, while bamboo and imitation bamboo became fashionable.

This medley of revivalist motifs produced much furniture which was extravagant and heavy; ornamentation in the shape of sphinxes, crocodiles, serpents, masks, eagles' heads, and dragons, was everywhere.

Many Regency pieces are, however, charming to our eyes. Many chairs had simple, Classical outlines, with front legs often curved in a sweeping scimitar shape, arms set high on the back and rounded forward in a scroll, and the back rail often curved for comfort. These chairs had style and elegance, their feminine appearance is evocative of polished society in gracious drawing-rooms. They were used by ladies who wore flowing white lawn or muslin dresses with the waistline under the armpits, few underclothes, hair piled on tops of their heads *à la Grecque*, and sandals on their feet. They must have felt very cold in ill-heated, elegant London houses and muddy, unswept London streets, but that doubtless mattered less than being in the fashion and paying a tribute to all things Greek. Sometimes flowers were worn in the hair, and the bonnets were modelled on Grecian helmets.

Not everyone felt the need either for fashion's or politics' sake to sit on Greek or Egyptian chairs. Those which Thomas Chippendale the Younger made in 1812 for Stourhead, in Wiltshire, were bold, masculine pieces, made of mahogany and with the principal lines emphasised by gilding.

Papiermâché, known in Georgian times, became very popular during the Regency and even chairs were made of it. It was made in Birmingham and the process of manufacture was a simple one, the basic material being paper-pulp. This was prepared in moulds, subjected to heavy pressure, and when finally completed it was strong and durable. The basic shape was painted over with many coats of black varnish and then decorated with floral designs, and sometimes inlaid with mother-of-pearl. The fashion for papiermâché furniture and boxes went out in about 1860.

The sofa of the early nineteenth century is important in the development of seating and tells us of a gradual relaxation of manners. It grew from the eighteenth-century idea of linking two chairs together to give a single seat for two people, but before long it tended to be occupied by only one person. Posture for sitting had previously been restricted to the vertical or near-vertical, but now became nearer the horizontal. Chaises-longues had tended to be used only by invalids and the elderly, and if anyone else reclined in public in a similar way they were thought very daring and advanced. In Jane Austen's *Mansfield Park*, Mrs Norris complains that it is 'a shocking trick for a young person to be always lolling on a sofa'. But loll they evidently did, for sofas were made in large quantities.

They were often called 'Turkey' sofas, or 'Ottomans' – again an echo of the Greek revolt against the Turks. These pieces had no back or sides, and were frequently of rosewood, or of beech painted or grained to imitate rosewood; the upholstery was covered in silk, often striped. Many other elegant examples had curved, rolled ends and back, and short outwardly curving legs in the form of lions' paws.

Ackerman's *Repository* published in 1809 shows drawings of sofas in a library, which suggests that this room was now being invaded by women and was no longer the masculine stronghold it had been.

Mrs Carlyle wrote charmingly to her husband, during one of his absences, telling him of the purchase of a sofa: 'You shall share the possession. Indeed, as soon as you perceive its vastness, its simple greatness, you will perceive that the thought of you was actively at work in my choice.' And some years later, in 1843, she wrote reporting 'I have realised an ideal,

50 A room in a Regency house, showing an 'Ottoman', a fire-screen, and a Regency chair

have actually acquired a small sofa!!'

After about 1830 the front legs of both chairs and sofas tended to be straight and turned, but the back legs kept the Regency curve for some time. The majority of Victorian chairs were upholstered, either with buttoning all over the seat, arms, and back, or with a back panel in a carved frame, with buttoned upholstery inside it.

Fashionable dining-chairs were stuffed with horsehair and covered in a black, shiny material made of woven horsehair. This would be unbearable for us to sit on nowadays, but we must remember that nineteenth-century men, women, and children were well protected by many layers of garments!

Comfort was more in demand than ever before. Manufacturers began to produce chair seats which were deeper from front to back, in order to provide greater comfort than could be obtained either by lolling sideways on a sofa or sitting upright on a chair shallow from front to back. Coiled springs were patented in 1828 and within a few years their use altered the line of seating. Springs need depth and the thickness in the seat which resulted from their use was balanced by increasing thickness of the arms; upholstery had sometimes enveloped the framework of chairs in the eighteenth century, now it began almost to envelop the sitter so that chairs and sofas could be sat *in*, not *on*. Elegant ease was replaced by opulent comfort.

Victorian women had time to kill and they spent a good deal of it in doing needlework of various kinds. Chairs, cushions, antimacassars,[1] footstools, and sofas were covered in petit-point, satin-stitch, or beaded embroidery. The introduction of analine dyes resulted in more strident colours, such as Prussian blue and chrome-yellow. These new dyes gradually replaced the earlier, more subtle, tones of vegetable dyes and gave a harsher look to clothes, wallpapers, curtains, and upholstery.

William Morris's influence gradually revolutionised advanced taste, in furniture and in much else. 'The Red House' which his friend, the architect Philip Webb designed for him and his new wife in 1860, set a new direction to the thinking of the intelligentsia about design. Before this, the kitchen in large houses had been in the basement; Webb put it on the ground floor, close to the dining-room. And the furniture, too, was sensible, practical, honest stuff, and from then onwards there was a definite distinction between furniture that was fashionable in society and furniture that was appreciated in advanced artistic circles. Highly polished mahogany remained high fashion, but among people of aesthetic tastes it was replaced by ebonised woods, unpolished light oak, and woods stained green, dark blue, or black. The legs of 'art' chairs were slender and turned, and carving was replaced by painting.

Walter Crane wrote of Morris's home:

> Plain white or green paint for woodwork drove wood-graining and marbling to the public house. The simple old Buckingham elbow chair, with its rush-bottomed seat was substituted for the wavy-backed, curly-legged and stuffed chair of the period. Rich or simple flat patterns acknowledged the walls and expressed the proportion of the room.

Among the craftsmen who were inspired by Morris's teachings were four who made simple, dignified furniture

---

[1] To lay over chair backs to protect them from the macassar oil which the men used in abundance to keep their hair smooth.

during the last decade of the century: Ernest Gimson, Sidney and Ernest Barnsley, and C. F. A. Voysey. They abhorred sham and overdecoration and their furniture was beautifully made, simple, and distinguished, without any of the vulgar overstatement current in fashionable pieces of their time. Some of their early pieces seem a little over-heavy to our eyes; they used solid wide boards and showed the joints of their wood prominently, but they were revolutionaries and much of what they made was intended as a protest against prevailing taste.

Morris's favourite dictum gradually opened people's eyes and awakened the consciences of a few thoughtful people:

> Have nothing in your home that you do not know to be useful or believe to be beautiful.

Tables

Early in the century, circular tables were fashionable, in small sizes as occasional-tables and larger for use in the breakfast-room and library. They had a central plinth with legs finishing in scroll feet, or a pedestal with four shorter legs curving outwards. In Victorian pedestal-tables the central support was often bulbous and heavy, with legs crudely carved.

At this time, several patents for extending dining-tables were taken out, but none of them proved entirely satisfactory. In his *Cabinet Dictionary* of 1803, Thomas Sheraton wrote:

> Common useful dining tables are upon pillar and claws, generally four claws to each pillar, with brass castors . . . between each of them is a loose flap, fixed by means of iron straps and buttons, so that they are easily taken off and put aside.

Circular dining-tables, too, were sometimes provided with an ingenious extension. The table was enlarged at the circumference, an additional 'ring' being supported on brackets which could be pulled out from under the centre.

There were many other types of table, large and small; sofa-tables were still in use; work-tables on stands had pleated silk pouches underneath and fitted drawers above; papier-mâché tea-tables and work-tables were popular and side-tables were made to stand in front of the window with potted ferns on them.

51 An early Victorian family scene. In the background a large bookcase, a work-table, fire-irons, and a lamp can be seen

The living-rooms of well-to-do people were furnished with an informality unknown in the previous century. Work-tables, small occasional-tables, and nests of tables, called 'trio' or 'quartetto' tables, stood about the room with apparent abandon. The authoress Fanny Burney expressed the opinion that no room was

> really comfortable, or even quite furnished, without two tables – one to keep the wall and take upon itself the dignity of a little tidyness, the other to stand here, there, and everywhere, and hold letters and make the place agreeable.

When Fanny was furnishing a small cottage for herself in 1801, she wrote to her father, Dr Burney, and asked him for a small table as a present – 'a sort of table for a little work and a few books, *en gala* – without which, a room looks always forlorn'.

Mahogany and satinwood were popular during most of the century, and boldly striped woods – amboyna, calamander, zebra wood, and kingwood – were imported from Brazil. When Napoleon forbade any of his European allies to import English goods or harbour English ships, many of our manufacturers found a way through this 'Continental System' and developed new markets in South America.

Maria Edgeworth, writing in 1820, mentioned having seen at Aston Hall, Birmingham, 'some fine tables of Mr. Bullock's making, one of wood from Brazil – zebra wood, and no more to be had for love or money'. George Bullock was a well-known cabinet-maker and sculptor who lived and worked in Liverpool and in London. He also popularised marble inlay and brass marquetry, known as 'English buhl', a fashion inspired by the fondness of the Prince Regent for the early eighteenth-century furniture made by A.-C. Boulle, ébéniste to Louis XIV, with its inlay of brass and also of silver and tortoiseshell on ebony. (See page 63.)

In the first decade of the century interest became aroused in the use of 'French' polish. We do not know who it was who first introduced the French polishing process into England, but before long it became fashionable to strip fine pieces and re-polish them.

The introduction of French polishing, and the increasing tendency to overload furniture with brass ornamentation are further indications of a decline in standards. Before the nineteenth century the maker of furniture produced his own designs, usually carrying out the wishes of his customers, but now designing and making and selling gradually became separate and the standards of all three declined. As Sir Gordon Russell vividly puts it:

> So long as furniture was made in the back shop and sold in the front shop, the seller knew what was of good quality and could convince the customer that it was worth paying for. But directly furniture was produced in a factory and distributed in retail shops, it became much simpler to sell on price instead of quality, which is impossible to explain without a real knowledge of construction.[1]

It was mainly in the middle- and upper-class homes that the new, flabby, over-ornamented furniture was to be found. Most homes in both town and country were so poor that little that we would call furniture existed at all; what there was was shoddy and lacking in grace, but had the virtue of being simple. Writing in *Cottage Economy*, issued in monthly parts during 1821, William Cobbett wrote that household goods should be

---

[1] *Designer's Trade*, Gordon Russell.

'warm, strong and durable' and that they should be handed on from generation to generation . . . 'In short, when a house is once furnished with sufficient goods, there ought to be no renewal of hardly any part of them wanted for half an age, except in case of destruction by fire.'

By the end of the century, skilled workers were living more comfortably, according to a report by Rowntree on conditions in York:

> The houses usually contain five rooms and a scullery. . . . The sitting room often contains a piano and an overmantel in addition to the usual furniture. . . . It is chiefly used on Sundays, or as a receiving-room for visitors who are not on terms sufficiently intimate to be asked into the kitchen. Occasionally it is used by the husband when he has writing to do . . . or by the children when practising music. The real living room is the kitchen, rendered cheerful and homely by the large open grate and the good oven, unknown in the south, but familiar in the north of England where coal is cheap, and where the thrifty housewife bakes her own bread. A sofa, albeit of horse-hair or American cloth, an arm-chair, a polished table, and china ornaments on the high mantlepiece, add the subtle touch of homeliness. . . .

Storage

During the Regency period, several new items of storage furniture appeared in English homes. George Smith, in his *Household Furniture* referred to cabinets, secretaries, revolving bookcases, sideboards, chiffoniers, and davenports.

The chiffonier was intended to stand in the drawing-room and served to house 'such books as are in constant use, or not of sufficient consequence for the library'. We also read of them being used to hold bowls of sweetmeats and fruit. In fact it was a multi-purpose piece; the name derived from the French word meaning 'rag-gatherer'!

The earliest types, small, delicate pieces with tapering legs and receding shelves at the top for displaying porcelain, were very different from the ugly Victorian versions which followed.

Victorian chiffoniers were indistinguishable from sideboards; they were massive pieces, often with marble tops,[1] ornately carved cupboard doors, and a mirror back with a carved frame. They reflected the flamboyant taste and prosperous conditions of the time; they were no longer something

---

[1] Steam-driven marble-cutting machines were available in the 1830s, so marble tops became much less expensive.

that had been designed to serve a practical purpose, but were in themselves the object of attention and admiration; they had become 'household gods', symbols of the owner's wealth and power, and were no longer household equipment.

Soon after Victoria's accession in 1839, a romantic revival in literature, added to the prevalent interest in medieval antiquities, had a marked effect upon domestic styles. The novels of Walter Scott were widely read and gave rise to a Gothic-Baronial influence in both architecture and furniture, named the 'Abbotsford' style, after Sir Walter's Gothic house in the Border country. Pointed arches, pinnacles, tracery, and ecclesiastical figures sprouted in the most unlikely places; the high tide of this Gothic Revival produced Barry's new House of Commons and St Pancras Station in London, the Town Hall in Manchester, Glasgow University, and much furniture like the cabinet by Pugin shown below. This was a time of great religious ferment; the determination of many radicals to reform the Established Church was opposed by the Oxford Movement, and 'Gothic' styles became strangely associated with ethics and Christian beliefs.

It is also strange that, at a time when ostentation and effect were a prime consideration in the minds of well-to-do house-

52 A cabinet designed by Pugin in neo-Gothic style, 1851. The carving is lavish, but notice the delicate work in the hinges of the doors

holders, veneering went out of favour. This had been a highly skilled and much-appreciated form of surface decoration in the late seventeenth and eighteenth centuries, but now, for a time, people began to dislike it and to think of the process as a dishonest way of covering up cheap and shoddy work with a showy top layer. This change of view arose not only because fashion is always changing and people rarely appreciate what their parents liked, but also because Charles Dickens wrote disparagingly of veneering and strengthened the growing prejudice against it. In *Our Mutual Friend* he described a showy, rather inferior couple as the Veneering Family:

> Mr. and Mrs. Veneering were bran-new people in a bran-new house in a bran-new quarter of London. Everything about the Veneerings was spick and span new. All their furniture was new, all their friends were new, all their servants were new, their plate was new, their carriage was new, their harness was new, their horses were new, their pictures were new, they themselves were new, they were as newly married as was lawfully compatible with their having a bran-new baby and if they had set up a great-grandfather, he would have come home in matting from the Pantechnicon, without a scratch upon him, French polished to the crown of his head.

There can be no doubt that Dickens disapproved of veneering!

China-cabinets with glazed doors were indispensable in any well-furnished room; the whatnot was a dainty stand, about 3 or 4 feet high, with several shelves, and was beloved by Victorian families for the display of wax flowers under glass domes, ships in bottles, glass paper-weights, and other treasured ornaments.

In 1856, a collection of Japanese woodcuts was discovered in Paris; art lovers throughout Europe became passionate admirers of Japan, exhibitions of Japanese art were held in Paris and London and it became 'the thing' to have bamboo and other furniture in a Japanese style. The Pre-Raphaelites, William Morris and the Art Workers' Guild found the simplicity of Japanese art much to their liking, and between 1860 and 1880 E. W. Godwin was designing thin and delicate furniture in the Japanese taste. Whistler's house, which was built for him by Godwin, had white and rich yellow walls, Japanese matting on the floors, plain curtains in straight folds, some pieces of Chinese porcelain, and a few simply framed pictures and etchings. Japan remained the strongest foreign influence on English design from the 1870s to the end of the century. Gilbert and Sullivan mocked the Japanese craze in *The Mikado*. In *Patience*, subtitled *An Aesthetic Opera*, they poured scorn on lovesick maidens and idyllic poets and on the whole Aesthetic movement:

> A Japanese young man
> A blue and white young man ...
> A pallid and thin young man
> A haggard and limp young man
> A greenery-yallery, Grosvenor Gallery
> Foot-in-the-grave young man.

The array of delicate pieces of furniture in between the more solid pieces of any Victorian drawing-room must have made life very difficult for any child allowed there. For dogs the situation was even worse, as we see from sound advice about Visiting, given by Mrs Beeton in the 1861 edition of her *Book of Household Management*:

> It is not advisable at any time to take a favourite dog into another lady's drawing-room, for many persons take an absolute dislike to such animals, and besides this, there is always a chance of a breakage of some article occurring through their leaping and bounding here and there, sometimes very much to the fear and annoyance of the hostess.

A davenport was a small, kneehole writing-desk, first made by the firm of Gillow for a Captain Davenport. Repeat orders for this type of desk were recorded in the firm's books as 'davenport desks'. Later the name was sometimes used in the United States to describe an upholstered sofa, and a couch which could be extended to form a bed.

A canterbury, which at the end of the eighteenth century was a supper-tray – a forerunner of the modern trolley-table – was by now a small stand with divisions, designed to hold books, atlases, or music. In *The Cabinet Dictionary* of 1803, Sheraton wrote that this kind of piece was so-called because the Archbishop of Canterbury first gave an order for one.

The music canterbury stood at the side of the piano for frequent use. Musical evenings were popular in middle-class homes, as a later writer described in his reminiscences:

The Musical Evening was a free-and-easy affair. . . . People . . . brought their music with them in a little music-case, mostly of patent leather. This they left in the hall with their hats and coats, or in the bedroom with their wraps, according to their sex. They seldom took it straight into the drawing-room with them. It was not good form to show that they were eager to perform, though it was the deadliest insult if their hostess forgot to ask them; they never went there again.[1]

The pianoforte had begun to be a most important piece of furniture during the Regency, and gradually replaced both the harp and the harpsichord. By the middle of the century the piano had become an essential mark of respectability and even small houses had one.

In Regency houses, bookshelves were often built into a room, low against a wall so that pictures could be hung over them. Small, free-standing bookcases, open in front, sometimes served as side-tables. Victorian bookcases were very large, with glazed doors, and many had a Gothic flavour in their decoration.

[1] *Twenty Shillings in the Pound,* MacQueen Pope.

53   The interior of a middle-class Victorian home, with children playing at 'Doctors', from a painting by F. D. Hardy

Many popular novelists published their stories in several volumes: Jane Austen's *Northanger Abbey* was issued in six parts and Dickens and Thackeray issued some of their novels in as many as twenty or twenty-four parts. It was part of the richness of the Victorian home that it had room also for so many bound copies of magazines – particularly the *Chambers'* and *Strand Magazines*. Sir Arthur Conan Doyle first introduced Sherlock Holmes to a fascinated public in the *Strand Magazine* in 1891.

Beds

William Cobbett's view of bedroom requirements was very simple:

> As to beds and bedding, and other things of that sort, all ought to be good in their nature, of a durable quality, and plain in their colour and form.

This was probably not the aim or the daydream of any nineteenth-century family, whether rich or poor. In 1853 an American visitor to a large country-house wrote:

> Upstairs are any number of chambers and dressing-rooms, with immense four-posters and immense wardrobes and immense washstands, and the invariable toilette and writing tables, with chintz curtains to the bed and windows, and a small sofa covered with the same.[1]

This was the pattern of the well-to-do family bedroom; the comfort was maintained by innumerable servants who kept a coal fire burning in each room in winter, carried hot water upstairs morning and evening in immense brass or copper cans, or filled a bath set before the fire, with towels warming alongside. Here the visitor could retire to write letters or read, before changing for dinner.

The Post in 1874 drew attention to new 'Art Furniture'[2] being made by C. Trapnell of Bristol:

> ... [Mr Trapnell's furniture] meets the most limited purse, whilst it is also quite up to the most princely requirements, and in every example from the highest to the lowest there runs the golden thread of an educated taste and a freshness and originality which few furniture manufacturers possess. ...

[1] Quoted in *Hospitable England*, Henry Dana.   [2] See also p. 111.

At that time an 'educated taste' did not, of course, imply an appreciation of simplicity or austerity. It was a taste for history, and for romantic reminiscence, as we may gather from the continuation of the article in *The Post*:

> The articles comprise a suite of pitch pine bedroom furniture, decorated with purple ornament in the Early English style. . . . A Gothic brass half-tester bedstead, with circular cornice, relieved with semi-arched coronals and hung with tapestry draperies.

However grand the bedroom, cleanliness, as we understand it, was difficult to maintain, even with an army of servants. Mrs Thomas Carlyle who, though not wealthy, mixed in the best intellectual and social circles recorded proudly, in 1835, the year of their installation at Cheyne Row, Chelsea: 'We have no bugs yet to the best of my knowledge; and I do not know of one other house among all my acquaintance that so much can be said for.' However, in 1842 she found that the kitchen bed 'is impregnated with these small beings'. She sold it and 'went the same day and bought a little iron bedstead for the kitchen for one pound two and sixpence'.

Mrs Beeton had much to say about cleaning bedrooms, and changing curtains and covers during the great spring clean. It is an indication of the rising standard of living in more modest homes that, during the 1880s, publishers began to issue booklets on housewifery, and more and more magazines contained articles about domestic discipline and economy. *The Economical Housewife*, published in 1882, stressed that the order and cleanliness of the house depend on the housemaids. The writer did not recommend a daily charwoman for she would charge a shilling a day, drink gin, and gossip! Another article, in the same magazine, gave careful directions for the weekly turning out of rooms and the getting rid of fleas, flies, and bugs in the beds.

These pamphlets were certainly written mainly for lower-middle-class housewives, so we can imagine something of the apalling conditions of dirt and overcrowding in the homes of the poor. Canon Barnett, who started his work in Whitechapel in 1872, saw his Christian mission in very human terms, and did an enormous amount to provide interest, education, and entertainment for his parishioners. Many of his wealthy friends received groups in their homes on parish outings and when, at one great house, the women were taken to a bedroom to leave their outdoor clothes, a small child remarked: 'Look, mother, here's a bed with a room to itself!'

When William Morris married the beautiful Jane, who had sat as a model for Rossetti and himself, they found that the furniture and furnishings available at the time were so distasteful that he and his friends set to work to create pieces that met their ideals. A local carpenter was employed to make up their designs, all 'as firm and heavy as a rock'. In designing for simplicity and honesty, they seemed to forget the need, which many other people had, for a degree of comfort. Sir Edward Burne-Jones's grand-daughter, Angela Thirkell, has written of the many holiday visits paid to her grandparents:

> As for the pre-Raphaelite beds, it can only have been the vigour and perfect health of their original designers that made them believe their work was fit to sleep on, for the foundation was of wooden slats.

The inventiveness of the time showed itself even in small domestic changes. Early in the century, traditional rocker-cradles were more and more superseded by swinging cots and an attempt was made to replace traditional rocker-maids by mechanical swingers. In his *Cabinet Directory* Sheraton described a swinging crib-bed, made by a cradle-maker of Long Acre, London. The cot, with simple balusters round it, was uncluttered and hygienic and an ingenious clockwork mechanism kept it swinging for forty-five minutes at one winding.

At the Great Exhibition, a papiermâché cot, named the 'Victoria Regia' was shown. The *Art Journal Catalogue* described it:

> ... designed by Mr. Bell, the eminent sculptor. The body of the cot is nautilus-shaped; it is of a dark tint, upon which is richly emblazoned the rose, nightshade, and poppy. The flowers of the Victoria Regia decorate the base, and gracefully curve over the cot as supports for the curtain. The entire fittings are sumptuous in character, but in the best possible taste.

The interest of the design to us is that the papiermâché was not used as imitation wood, but treated as a moulded plastic – nearly a hundred years before the existence of moulded plastic as we understand it.

The Victorians were proud of their achievements, both great and small, whether material, social, or political. They firmly believed that there were still better times to come. In the *History of England*, which he wrote at this time, Macaulay forecast a future age when 'numerous comforts and luxuries which are now unknown, or confined to a few, may be within the reach of every diligent and thrifty working man'. Even Macaulay could not have imagined how great and how many the 'comforts and luxuries' of the succeeding century would be.

54 A page from a catalogue issued in 1896 by Oetzmann & Co., London. Notice the heavily upholstered furniture and abundance of decoration

7 *The Twentieth Century*

EVEN LORD MACAULAY could not have guessed how greatly human affairs would change in the twentieth century. The Victorian Age had been a great one for England; for almost a hundred years this country had been the most powerful in the world, and its enormous social achievements at home had been brought about without a revolution. English people knew they had set an example to the world, but now the future was less certain.

Although England had worked hard for her great position, her industries were not expanding as quickly as before and other nations were challenging her pre-eminence. The Germans and the Americans were the great scientists and inventors now, and they were beginning to capture England's trade in world markets.

At the beginning of the century, class divisions were very marked: the well-to-do led dignified, leisured lives with many servants to wait upon them, while the many poor families suffered greatly and lacked any kind of security. Lady Asquith described an aspect of London in the first decade of this century, as she remembered it when she was a child and her father Prime Minister:

> I can remember as a child being haunted by the beggars in the streets, the crossing-sweepers who held out their tattered caps for pennies, the children in rags, fluttering like feathers when the wind blew through them, the down-and-outs sleeping out under arches or on the benches in the parks with an old newspaper for cover. Those were the days when an agricultural labourer earned and brought up a family on thirteen shillings a week, when a worker in the towns earned eighteen shillings to a pound, to say nothing of the submerged mass of sweated workers down below. There was no insurance against sickness or unemployment, no old-age pensions with their promise of safety at the end of life, no net stretched beneath the feet of those who fell except that of sporadic charity and the workhouse.

Since those days, the average person's standard of living has improved out of all recognition and we can all buy and use things now which were only possible for a tiny minority before the First World War. The very poor have become steadily fewer and our attitude to poverty has completely changed. In previous centuries you were considered to be lazy or thriftless if you were poor, and this was still so in Edwardian times. Now, on the contrary, poverty has come to be regarded as a social disorder, a mistake in social organisation which can, in time, be put right.

During these seventy-odd years, everybody's horizons have become much wider than ever before. People not only go further and more quickly and more often, but they know much more about events in the world and hear about new ideas almost at once, so they think in a wider way also. Traditional ideas are not accepted as readily as before and innumerable things that have been taken for granted in the past are now questioned.

Two world wars have, of course, left their mark. England has changed from being a little island in control of a world-wide Empire, to being a small part of Europe, a member of a Commonwealth not all of whose members are friendly to the 'Mother' country.

Increasing mechanisation has meant better working conditions and more leisure for everybody. Most people can now read and write, but electronics have developed a system of communication which seems at times to make reading unnecessary. Telephones, radio, television, computers – all these recent inventions are important stages in a revolution affecting every part of our lives.

Perhaps the greatest change of all in our society in this century is the evident necessity for planning and control in many spheres which were previously left to chance or to individual effort. In this there are, of course, great benefits for us all, but great dangers also.

Building

In 1902 H. G. Wells wrote:

> Great towns before this century presented rounded contours and grew as a great puff-ball swells, the modern Great City looks like something that has burst an intolerable envelope and splashed.

All this new development was Late Victorian, most of it was unplanned, and seems dismal and unattractive to our eyes.

However, for innumerable English men and women these little homes were precious and had accommodation better than had ever before been available to middle-class people. This description of such suburban town-houses was written at the turn of the century:

> ... inside, there is a passage, a parlour, a back-room, a kitchen with a gas stove and a sink, electric light, two bedrooms upstairs, perhaps a bathroom, and certainly a separate and cleanly water-closet.

It was not, however, until 1909 that a new Housing Act gave Local Authorities power to fix the density of housing, and by then H. G. Wells's 'intolerable envelope' had become even more intolerable. In 1902, Ebenezer Howard's book, *Garden Cities of Tomorrow*, attracted the attention not only of architects and social reformers, but of many speculative builders, who applied the name to almost any housing scheme where a few original trees survived. The Garden Cities of Letchworth, Hampstead, and Welwyn influenced the planning and development of municipal housing estates both at home and abroad. A new form of romantic, cosy house became popular; suburban villas began to look like enlarged cottages. Sash-windows, with large plate-glass panes, were replaced with casements with 'leaded lights', and in the front door a panel of stained glass, or 'bull's eyes' of glass were framed in wood or lead.

When glass had been blown by hand, such 'bull's eyes' were the thick lumps of molten glass which stuck to the glass-blower's long pipe as the material gradually cooled. In the seventeenth and eighteenth centuries, many people had been glad to have them in their windows because they were cheaper than the smooth pieces from the edge of the blown circle of glass, and because there was nothing better available. The Victorians had often used cheap materials and mechanical methods in order to imitate costly and elaborate details; strangely, the Edwardian householder, living in an artistic 'garden' suburb, went to any amount of trouble and expense to imitate materials which had, in earlier times, been considered cheap but adequate.

Although an enormous amount of house-building was done by speculative builders at the beginning of the century, several talented architects were also at work. Charles Rennie Mackintosh, the Scot, was the first British architect to design houses in an entirely new manner, not derived from any period style. His Glasgow School of Art built between 1896 and 1909 is still a building of simple originality. Mackintosh himself wrote, in 1900:

> How absurd it is to see modern churches, theatres, banks, museums, exchanges, municipal buildings and art galleries made in the imitation of Greek temples.

Other outstanding architects were Sir Edwin Lutyens, Norman Shaw, and C. F. A. Voysey, who all built individual houses of charm and simplicity and used traditional materials honestly. Lutyens and Shaw built many brick houses in neo-Georgian styles; Voysey was more original. His plans were informal, his elevations plain and clear-cut, with bold, bare walls, small windows, and steep roofs with tall chimneys. His houses were designed as buildings to be lived in and not merely to be looked at, though they are indeed well worth the looking, especially his own house at Chorley Wood in Hertfordshire, built in 1900.

There was a building boom before the First World War; small houses all over the country were built in 'Tudor' style; stained slats of wood were nailed on to the face of brickwork, to imitate fifteenth- and sixteenth-century timber-framing; every little villa had to look like a Tudor mansion in miniature, with a gable crowning its projecting bay-window.

During the First World War, the men in the services were promised by Lloyd George's government 'homes fit for heroes to live in' and, afterwards a number of Local Authorities employed architects to plan simple and agreeable houses in housing estates, though not enough of them to satisfy the demand.

During the '20s and '30s, ribbon-building along main roads was undertaken by speculative builders, many of whom had neither taste nor ideals. All over the country, in the name of 'development', trees were felled, old properties demolished, and cheap, jerry-built, badly planned houses were put up. Here is an amusing picture, by Osbert Lancaster, of the worst kind of speculative building:

55 The Orchard, Chorley Wood, designed by C. F. A. Voysey in 1900. The design is simple and practical, and relies on the honest use of traditional materials

56 An Art Nouveau dining-room at the turn of the century. Every surface is decorated in an exaggerated style

While he is heavily indebted to history for the majority of his decorative and structural details (in almost every case the worst features of the style from which they were filched), in the planning and disposition of his erections the speculative builder displays a genius that is all his own. Notice the skill with which the houses are disposed, that ensures that the largest possible area of countryside is ruined with the minimum of expense; see how carefully each householder is provided with a clear view into the most private offices of his next-door neighbour and with what studied disregard of the sun's aspect the principal rooms are planned.

Local Authorities had legal powers to plan both town and country areas, but hesitated to use these powers because public opinion still considered that individual liberty and private property were sacrosanct. However, a number of large municipal slum-clearance schemes were begun and these produced new, inexpensive homes of a much higher standard than before. But no working-class estates or blocks of flats were built in the modern style until the late 1930s.

'The Modern Movement' was being developed in Europe as a new, cosmopolitan architectural style before the First World War. In 1901 the American architect, Frank Lloyd Wright, had issued a *Manifesto on Art and the Machine*, a clarion call to try to link the ideals of the Arts and Crafts pioneers to the reality of machine production. Soon after the war the new revolutionary style became fashionable in England among intellectuals and among a few leaders of society. This twentieth-century style has affected the making of nearly everything ever since.

The impetus came from Germany, where architectural giants such as Walter Gropius, Marcel Breuer, Mies van der Rohe, and the Frenchman, Le Corbusier, had been working in a new and stimulating design school in Weimar – the Bauhaus. There, teachers were working out logical and creative ways of training designers to design for machine production. Gropius was Director of the Bauhaus, where he and his colleagues studied new methods of manufacture, particularly the use of glass and steel in simple, functional ways. In 1933 Hitler closed the Bauhaus and many of its members fled from Germany to the United States; some came to Britain on the way but opinion here was less sympathetic to new ideas. Many of the best examples of house design in this country in the '30s resulted from the co-operation of Bauhaus refugees with our own architects. Gropius came in 1934–36 and his collaboration with Maxwell Fry produced houses and flats of great distinction (his Sun House in Hampstead was one of the first open-plan houses in this country); Erich Mendelsohn, Serge Chermayeff, Marcel Breuer, and Berthold Lubetkin, too, had a dynamic influence upon the younger British architects and a group of them formed 'Tecton', a famous firm which designed a number of fine houses in those experimental years, as well as Zoo buildings and High Point flats in Highgate.

New materials and new techniques were now available to architects for the first time. The use of steel and concrete meant that roofs and balconies could be cantilevered out with no pillars to support them, open-plan interiors were now possible, and external walls were non-weightbearing so that large areas of glass were a possibility.

However, English people are conservative and were slow to accept the new style of building for domestic purposes. Some of the best of the new buildings in the '30s were factories, hospitals, airports, and railway stations, in which architects were able to consider, first and foremost, the purpose of the building, without being handicapped by sentiment or by a concern for past styles.

The Second World War created enormous problems for architects and town-planners. Methods of building were modified as a result of wartime lessons in aircraft production, and the prefabricated houses put up as a temporary measure were better planned than many previously built in traditional ways.

The Town and Country Planning Act of 1947 was an attempt to ensure that the mistakes of the '30s were not repeated, and the New Towns Act brought into being a major experiment in domestic housing. There are still areas in which poor standards are accepted, but much well-designed, beautifully proportioned, and well-sited architecture has been built during recent years. A number of able young architects have turned their attention to speculative building, and have shown that nowadays this term need no longer imply poor design, shoddy workmanship, or a slavish copying of historic styles.

Rooms

It is seldom that the turn of a century serves also as a turning-point in the arts, but this was the case at the turn of this century. The revolution which had been brewing for a long time in the minds of British architects and craftsmen began to manifest itself in furnishings in the years after 1900. But for a few years still, an irrelevant, very exaggerated style of decoration was high fashion and delayed the development of the modern movement.

In England, this new style was first known as 'New Art', and seemed to be a logical development of the 'Art Movement' of the 1880s. It was a curvy, asymmetrical style, with every surface packed with ornament. Writhing leaves and stems wound over wallpapers, mantelpiece, curtains, furniture, fireplaces, glassware, and even book illustration. 'Art Nouveau' was much more in vogue in France, Belgium, Austria, and Spain than in this country. Many English designers adopted a puritanical view and condemned the precious, elegant, totally impractical products of the new style. Walter Crane, a disciple of William Morris, referred to 'that strange decorative disease known as L'Art Nouveau' and when, in 1900, some foreign objects in this style were presented to the Victoria and Albert Museum, a letter of protest was sent to *The Times* by a group of architects with Arts and Crafts sympathies. They described the objects as 'lacking in regard for the materials employed', and they despised those who worked in the style because of their individualism and lack of social conscience.[1]

But the pioneer architects and craftsmen of Edwardian times had far more than the excesses of Art Nouveau to worry them. The furniture trade and the public had seriously misinterpreted their teachings; the devotion of the Movement to medieval craftsmanship aroused an interest in the Middle Ages and led to a craze for antiques which could only be satisfied by providing reproductions of original period designs. The public appetite for fakes was insatiable and the trade was quick to exploit the demand for any and every style. Reproduction panelling was sold by unscrupulous firms as genuine, and put up in innumerable dining-rooms all over the country.

A writer in *House and Garden* in 1921 commented:

> ... in every town in England, shops filled with every sort of second-hand junk have multiplied and people utterly devoid of taste proudly display their 'finds'; throughout the middle classes an

---

[1] Art Nouveau curves are still seen here and there on fireplaces, on banisters, and stained glass. During the late '60s the style was resurrected, linked with 'pop' art and used on fabrics, carrier-bags, posters, and even in lettering.

'old' thing has become synonymous with a thing that is beautiful and desirable. . . .

Salesmen, of course, had a vested interest in period styles and had good reason to discourage any tendencies on the part of their clients to seek modern furniture, which they could not supply. A conventional home of the '20s and '30s had living-rooms which were a pastiche of Tudor and Georgian interiors: the drawing-room was furnished with eighteenth-century furniture, either real or fake, the dining-room panelled in oak, with a 'Tudor' table and leather-covered oak chairs, and curtains of a chintz reproduction of Elizabethan embroidery.

In 1922 the discovery by Lord Carnarvon of the tomb of Tutankhamen aroused an interest in Egyptian art comparable to that caused by the publications of the archaeologists Napoleon took with him on his Egyptian campaign, more than a century before. It was almost as romantic as finding a lost city and had an effect upon jewellery, dress, interior decoration, and architecture: the rich personal belongings of the young Pharaoh were reproduced on wallpapers and curtain fabrics, and there was a short-lived vogue for reproductions of the furniture found in the tomb.

The British Empire Exhibition at Wembley in 1924, of which the Wembley Stadium is a permanent relic, had a long-term effect upon the appearance of English rooms. At the Exhibition there was a display of a great many exotic colonial woods, which attracted much attention. The long pre-eminence of oak, walnut, and mahogany was undermined and, in the succeeding years, coloured woods with unusual grains gradually became popular.

To be really in fashion in the '20s and early '30s, rooms had to be decorated in the 'jazz' manner, a style inspired by the angular forms of Cubist art which had now spread beyond the circle of Picasso and Braque. The smart shape was the triangle, which was seen in electric light shades, mirrors, windows, furniture, wireless sets, and clocks. The diagonal cutting-off of corners was chic and the 'rising sun' was a popular motif which can still be seen here and there on cinema façades and on many a suburban garden gate. This style is also known as 'Art Déco', a name derived from the great Paris exhibition of 1925, the 'Exposition Internationale des Arts Décoratifs et Industriels Modernes'.

There were still enough rich people to have things personally made and designed for them and to enjoy decoration for decoration's sake, but this thoughtless state of affairs came to an end with the Wall Street slump. After 1931 the Jazz Age drifted away, on a tide of shifting social and political events, from a world depression to a second war.

The true modern spirit of the time had been developing in Germany, as we have seen, and began slowly to have an effect in this country. While the majority of English living-rooms were an imitation of those in Tudor mansions or Georgian country-seats, a few *avant-garde* designers were selling the 'Bauhaus' style to a very few intellectuals of mainly left-wing revolutionary views. Those who were in sympathy with the new continental style bought carpets, light fittings, glass, china, and fabrics which completely changed the look of their traditionally built rooms. While most manufacturers continued to play safe and the majority of customers continued to buy 'period' designs, those who were looking ahead tended to feel themselves missionaries for a new way of life. Le Corbusier had called a house 'a machine for living in' many years before and, now, austerity was taken to greater and greater lengths as walls were stripped of paper, pictures became taboo, and pattern was only acceptable on rugs. A revolution, in taste as in anything else, always results in extremes. Now, in the 1970s, the pendulum has swung back a little, but the majority of rooms in the majority of homes in this country probably look remarkably like those of the intellectual élite who were sneered at for their extreme taste in the '30s.

Since the Second World War there have been great changes in the layout of houses and the tendency now is to have fewer rooms than before. Even small houses often have a 'through' living-room, a dining-kitchen, or an entirely open plan. In a sense, the modern mass-produced home shows a return to the communal living of the medieval hall, except that modern heating and lighting, glass walls and sliding partitions give wide freedom of choice in the use of space.

Furniture

The pace of change in our twentieth century is only matched by the degree of change and its pervasiveness. For this and other reasons it does not seem appropriate to subdivide a consideration of furniture into its different purposes, as was done in previous chapters. Things are both simpler and more involved nowadays and political theories and social moralities enter into the story.

Reproduction Furniture

We may think that the Victorians showed bad taste in their more ostentatious furniture, but it was a positive taste, appropriate to the spirit of their age. Much of the furniture made during the first half of our twentieth century, on the other hand, was a shoddy imitation of the 'antique'.[1] The medieval flavour of so many of the Arts and Crafts products had captured the public imagination and designers and manufacturers merely copied old styles, instead of trying to make pieces suitable to twentieth-century people, leading twentieth-century lives.

In 1906 C. F. A. Voysey, in a pamphlet entitled *Reason as a Basis of Art*, wrote:

> The desire for gaudy richness and effect has produced the shams we find in the shops. The well-made, solid, plain articles, such as the poor man, if he did not try to hide his poverty, would wish to have, are scarcely ever to be found. There is a universal desire (which is the outcome of insincerity) to make things look better than they are. The plain, solid oak furniture of bygone times is now replaced by stained and highly polished and decorated rubbish created by an endeavour to make something look better than it is. So-called ornament is lavishly used to hide bad workmanship and bad material. A general revolt against shams would surely check the supply. But even those who have an idea that they ought to like the plain article, show they are not wholly freed from the snare of sham by having it stained with a false age. It must look old to please them, even though it were made yesterday.

It is difficult for us to realise how limited was the choice of furniture available seventy years ago; everyone bought antiques if they could afford them, for there was nothing else to buy. Those of modest means either bought simple, second-hand pieces which had probably been used in the hall or the servants' rooms of larger Victorian houses, or they bought fakes.

---

[1] The word would have seemed absurd to any educated person in the past. It was first applied to furniture, when John Evelyn, in the seventeenth-century wrote in his diary of seats being 'carv'd à l' antique' – related to Classical Greek and Roman designs. The word 'ancient' was used in the early nineteenth century to describe works of remote antiquity and also medieval architecture and furniture. In Eastlake's *Hints on Household Taste* in 1878 'ancient' is used to describe old furniture, a writer in 1888 condemned the 'fabrication of antique furniture'; in this century it has come to mean any furniture over a hundred years old.

The post-war years in England also were not creative in furniture design. Designers were still shackled by tradition unthinkingly applied and were looking back to the past for inspiration. They were hampered by the ignorance and prejudice of customers, who still felt that an 'old' thing, or something pretending to be old, was preferable to anything else. In 1923, Gordon Russell wrote a leaflet about the morality of making fakes:

> 'Wonderful, isn't it? Only an expert would ever guess it wasn't old!' How often has one heard this remark made in a tone which leaves no doubt that the speaker considers it as a vast achievement, like the drawing which is 'just as good as a photograph'. But how many people who make similar exclamations ever pause to consider what they mean? Is there indeed so great a gulf fixed between the faking of houses and furniture and the faking of £5 notes? Are we to admire things because they are beautiful, or because they are old? The doctrine that nothing is beautiful unless it is old has created an army of swindlers, whose artful work may in time even bring discredit on the lovely craftsmanship which they attempt to imitate.

Raymond Mortimer, in *The New Interior Decoration*, explained some reasons why English design was so conservative at the end of the '20s:

> in England the rich are content to devote their fortunes to grouse moors and racing stables; if they buy a picture, it is by an artist who is safely dead; if they require a house they either buy an old one or order one that will look old, from an architect with a talent for pastiche . . . the absence of buildings in the modern style such as have spread over the Continent, has caused interior decoration in England to develop along peculiar lines.

Of course, standards of taste are always set by the wealthy, and it is understandable that modest families at that time copied the assumptions of the rich, by buying poor imitations of the antiques which lent such status to successful homes. Many thinking people in the '30s, however, laid the blame for the low level of craftsmanship and design in popular furniture upon the manufacturers, who were only concerned with profits and with avoiding payment for any original furniture designs. At this time hire-purchase payment arrangements were virtu-

57   A drawing-room of 1908. Every piece of furniture is reproduction!

58   Dining-room furniture designed in 1935 by R. D. Russell, and made in Gordon Russell's workshop. Natural woods, fine craftsmanship, and understated elegance contrast strongly with the room above

ally uncontrolled, which was yet another factor causing shoddy workmanship. The dark treacly stain then thought to give a 'rich Jacobean' look, very effectively covered poor workmanship and disguised inferior wood, and many purchasers were concerned with little beyond the size of their down-payment and the monthly charges. Since the Second World War, as we shall see, there has been a marked decline in interest in reproduction furniture, and even 'genuine' antiques are now bought for investment as often as for practical use.

Hand-made Furniture

It is doubtful if the work of the Arts and Crafts Movement has ever been fully appreciated. Here were educated men and women working with their hands, caring passionately about the use of good materials, honest craftsmanship, and modern design, at a time when everyone else – rich and less rich alike – were interested only in surrounding themselves with an atmosphere of past centuries. The artist-craftsmen believed that good design must start from a practical purpose, the workman was given as much credit as the designer, and making by hand was seen as making with joy. They hated the machine and all it stood for, they felt a renewed faith in the social message of art and craft.

Ernest Gimson was the greatest of the artist-craftsmen in the early years of this century. He and his colleagues did not imitate traditional styles, there was nothing 'olde worlde' about the furniture he made, much of which was so simple that it looks very much of our own day. He loved timber and always left it in its natural colour, rather than varnish or stain it, as was usual at the time. He was before his time, too, in his honesty in showing the structure of his pieces and in making drawer handles, locks, and hinges into simple, decorative shapes.

C. F. A. Voysey was a leader in the movement towards simplicity in domestic architecture and designed with wit and style the furniture, wallpapers, and fittings for his houses. The furniture was bold, simple, and direct, usually in unvarnished oak, often with cut-out heart shapes as decoration, and large handles or hinges, painted black.

Sidney and Ernest Barnsley worked with Ernest Gimson at first in London and then in the Cotswolds. Their furniture and their buildings were perfectly in the English tradition, without being at all imitative, and Edward Barnsley, son of Sidney, is still carrying on the same tradition of fine craftsmanship.

These men were giants, all of them fortunate that they had private means and could, therefore, afford to spend their lives making beautiful, expensive furniture, without being unduly concerned about economics. Such creative ability is, of course, enormously important in any society, but it was obvious, even then, that people's needs cannot be adequately met by hand production.

The Arts and Crafts Exhibition Society were still holding exhibitions of handwork in the '20s but these evoked little public interest. A critic wrote in *The Studio* in 1926:

> ... the general atmosphere is of sentimental loyalty to ideas and methods which provide no inspiration to the younger generation ... the galleries seem peopled with ghosts of the past.

It was a mistake; there could be no going back, and before long the arts and crafts had degenerated into the 'arty crafty', largely because of their 'other-worldliness'.

A different approach to the problem of art and craft in modern industrial society was expressed by the sculptor Eric Gill, one of the many modern artists much influenced by the ideas of William Morris. In 1934 he wrote:

> The problem of twentieth-century art is: how to arrange or organise the state so that the making of things shall be controlled by those who make them and those who use them, and removed from the control of those who merely sell them. The problem for those who are concerned for the good quality of things made (and that is the same as saying the problem confronting everybody) is the problem how to break the commercial spirit which now moves everyone, whether in big business or small, whether in high places or low.

Eric Gill saw clearly that the craftsman's attitude of mind, and the ageless pre-industrial way of working (a thing made by one person for another) are incompatible with the satisfaction of the needs of a large population. But he had no ready-made solution for the dangerous division.

During recent years there has been a renewal of interest in craftsmanship in the Western world. Perhaps this is because the mechanisation of modern life attracts many people to the individually made object; perhaps it is because leisure hours are greater than they used to be and handwork satisfying to more and more people; perhaps, too, it is because there is now official support for the crafts.

There are still idealists, working on their own or in small group workshops, producing fine hand-made furniture for sale to those who can afford to buy it. This creative work undoubtedly has great value for society, and for the craftsman himself, but he rarely earns a sufficient living by his craftsmanship alone, and may have to teach or lecture in order to be able to live at a reasonable standard. If he is successful he is beset with the problem of whether to expand and so risk losing the individuality in his work, and whether to use power-driven tools and so risk turning handwork into machinework.

A number of professional associations and two bodies, the Crafts Centre of Great Britain and the Crafts Council of Great Britain – both helped by small Government grants – exist to maintain close contact between craftsmen and the public, and to secure continuing recognition for craftsmanship. In a world where mass-production can provide a good material standard for everyone, the skilled craftsman, working individually, is still able to provide inspiration and stimulus for designers working in industry, and for society as a whole.

Machine-made Furniture

The followers of William Morris felt themselves to be missionaries, but they failed to deal with the fundamental problem of twentieth-century manufacture – how to use the machine in the best way for the work for which it is suitable. They considered the machine to be an enemy and did not seem to realise that it had come to stay and must be used to make everyday things in sufficient quantity for everyone to be able to have them.

It was Sir Ambrose Heal who first designed and sold machine-made pieces of good design. Heal and Sons had been producing Victorian furniture, until Ambrose Heal joined the family firm and began to design simple pieces in fumed or waxed, but unstained, oak. In 1898 the first catalogue of Heal's Plain Oak Furniture showed simple wooden bedsteads, without carving or other decoration. Since that time the firm has consistently sold modern furniture, both of designs commissioned by themselves and those produced by other manufacturers.

An attempt was made, in 1915, to bring about a closer understanding between art and industry, by founding the Design and Industries Association. The founders held the view that 'the disease of modern design and industry is not due to machinery, but to the imperfect comprehension of its limitations and its possibilities'.

The motto of the D.I.A. was 'Fitness for Purpose' and, after the war years, the Association tried to raise the standard of industrial design by holding exhibitions of good machine-made things, by publishing pamphlets and by sending speakers round the country.

Gordon Russell began to experiment in making modern furniture after the First World War. His father had repaired and sold antiques, but during his wartime experience Gordon Russell decided that he wanted to make new furniture. As he writes in his autobiography:

> I felt strongly that my generation, which had destroyed so much lovely work, had a constructive duty to perform; somehow or other we had to hand on to those coming after us good things of our own creation.... My working knowledge of old furniture gave me a respect for tradition, which I believe to be most important if one wants to see today's work in perspective. To me it was a poor age which could make no contribution of its own. I argued that if the eighteenth century had been content to imitate the seventeenth, then the finest age of English cabinetmaking would never have been born....

Gordon Russell was greatly influenced by Ernest Gimson, and much of his work has retained a certain rural flavour which is very much in the English tradition: natural woods, fine craftsmanship, and understated elegance. He was producing the best-designed English furniture in the '20s and '30s and there is no doubt that many of the pieces made by his firm then and now will be sought after by collectors in years to come, because of their intrinsic excellence.

However, the English public were little interested in new designs and leadership in furniture-making after the First World War passed to Germany and Scandinavia. Marcel Breuer first became known in the 1930s for his functional furniture, constructed of tubular steel and plywood. His use of bent tubular-steel framing in furniture has been described as 'the single most influential furniture invention in this century to date', and his first tubular-steel chair, made in 1926, was taut, light, and almost transparent. He named it the 'Vassily' chair, after the painter Vassily Kandinsky, who was a fellow worker at the Bauhaus. Breuer and his colleagues also experimented with laminated wood, and Mies van der Rohe's 'Barcelona' chair, made in 1929, was bought by wealthy people all over the world.

Steel and chromium-plated furniture was popular in *avant-garde* circles in this country during the late '20s, but was thought by many people to be too unfriendly and only suitable for use in cafés, bars, hospitals, and waiting-rooms.

Inevitably, the new furniture encountered hostile criticism from those who were preoccupied with the past. A writer in 1929 criticised '... these modernist rooms, the most impersonal or dehumanised that have ever been contrived....'

In 1931 attention was drawn to a new aspect of modern design, by staging an Exhibition of Swedish Decorative Art in London. The sparse, elegant simplicity of the furniture and the fabrics in the Exhibition had a tremendous impact upon the more receptive of the public, and upon the young in particular. They were beginning to feel no longer content to live in rooms reflecting the life of their parents or grandparents, but were attracted to surroundings which reflected the rapidly changing times.

Gradually, too, in the '30s, people began to think in less traditional terms about what pieces of furniture they needed. Wardrobes, which were heavy and cumbrous but showing only a slight resemblance to their historical counterparts, were abandoned by many younger people in favour of built-in cupboards. These cupboards, painted to match the walls of the room, were made possible by the new laminated woods which were becoming plentiful; they made rooms look larger and, of course, reduced the cost of furnishing a home.

Another piece of furniture which became less fashionable at this time was the washstand, formerly a necessity when a toilet-set of basin, water-jug, slop-pail, chamber-pot, and soap-dishes, all in decorated china, was found in every bedroom. Bathrooms in newly built houses and flats, and improvements in plumbing, made a washstand redundant, though older people still clung to its use.

The increasing taste for built-in furniture in new, smaller homes increased the popularity of the divan instead of the heavy iron or wooden bedstead. The settee, however, maintained its popularity as a central feature in the majority of living-rooms, where, with the addition of two upholstered easy-chairs, it became the 'three-piece suite'. This is still considered a necessity in many homes, though more and more manufacturers offer their customers a wider variety of seat furniture.

The idea of 'unit' furniture, so that the buyer could add to his set of cupboards or shelves when he could afford to, was introduced in the early '30s. A very practical scheme, this appealed particularly to those living in small flats and to people with small incomes.

An important new material developed in this country at the time was latex foam rubber. Used for upholstery, it is long-lasting, resilient, hygienic, and labour-saving; it is now so generally used that it is difficult to remember what chairs and mattresses felt like before it was on the market.

Two other important public exhibitions in the '30s widened the circle of those who were becoming interested in modern design. In 1933 the Design and Industries Association Exhibition at Dorland Hall showed advanced designs by younger British designers and interior decorators; in 1935 there was an important exhibition of Art in Industry at the Royal Academy. The Prince of Wales was Chairman of the Exhibition Committee. Not all the exhibits were in the new style, and there were complaints, as there had been in 1831, about the standard of some of them and the high prices; but interest in the Modern Movement was certainly widening.

During the '30s the Modern Movement suffered from the development of a type of mass-produced furniture known as 'modernistic'. This took the form of novelty for novelty's sake, and resulted from the intense financial competition at the cheaper end of the furniture trade. Every year saw minor variations in surface ornament: bulbous legs became mixed with 'jazz' triangles, a version of 'Knole' armchairs became three-piece 'suites', reproduction antique buffets and long-case clocks were made into cocktail cabinets, mirrors sprouted plastic tassels on their frames, handles were of carved chromium or glass, door panels of wardrobes were upholstered in satin or velvet – all in the name of novelty, of modernity, of profit. This was certainly the lowest ebb to which English furniture has ever sunk.

In a survey of department stores in the mid '30s, Dr Nikolaus Pevsner found that many manufacturers knew that they were selling rubbish, but excused themselves on the grounds that if the goods were well designed, the public would not buy them. This cynical, depressing point of view seemed all too true at the time; it took the shortages and efforts of wartime and of the post-war period to prove the gentlemen wrong.

Utility Furniture

During the Second World War supplies of timber, as of everything else, were desperately short. Imports were heavily restricted, labour was scarce, homes were being bombed and furniture destroyed, and newly married couples needed basic necessities to start their new homes. In 1942 the Board of Trade decided to provide a ration of new furniture for those in need of it, and the Utility Furniture Scheme was established.

Because of the acute timber shortage, the variety of furniture had to be limited, and there had to be restrictions on who could buy it, how large each ration could be, how much timber could be used in each piece, and the prices that could be charged. Most of the furniture-manufacturers were already fully occupied in making aircraft and other war supplies, but over a hundred firms were chosen to make Utility furniture to designs chosen by the Utility Panel.

The 'points' system of allocation was similar to that used for food and clothing, but a new and revolutionary idea was that in the case of furniture, the *design* should also be controlled. There was, of course, disagreement among members of the Utility Panel about the most suitable style for the new, controlled furniture. Some members thought that the public should be given 'what they liked', which was imitation antique furniture; others felt that nothing less than modern design would do. Fortunately, the latter group won the day, primarily because the shortage of timber meant that there was not enough for bulbous legs or fake carving.

Gordon Russell, who was a member of the Utility Panel, described the result of the decision:

59 The 'Barcelona' chair designed in 1929 by Mies van der Rohe

60 A milestone in the history of English furniture – a Utility bedroom suite of 1942

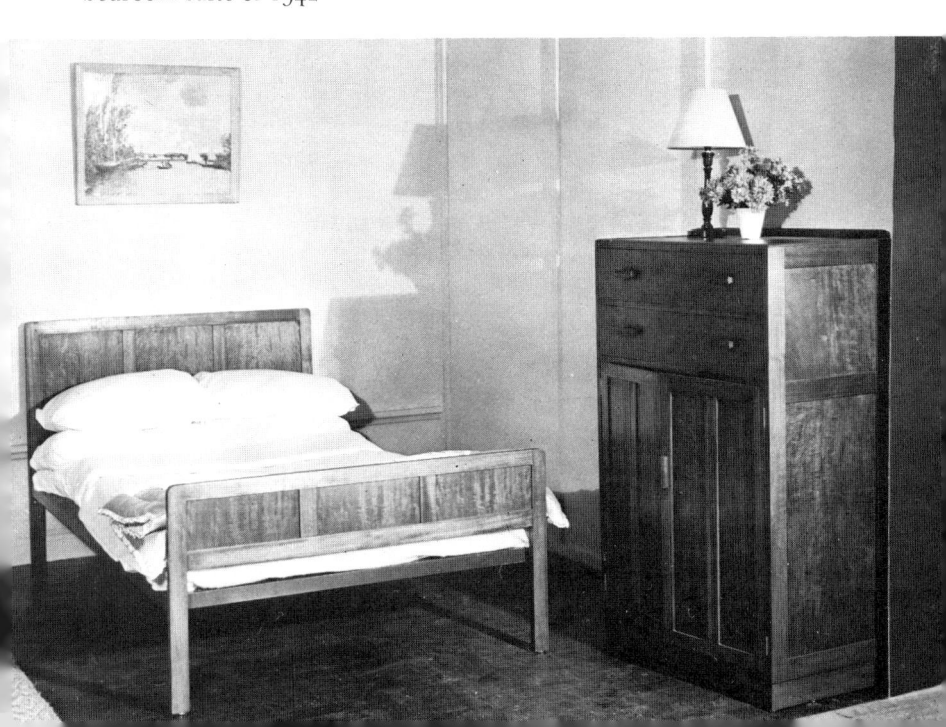

... It must have been a bit of a shock that a type of design which had been pioneered for years by a small minority – whilst the trade looked on and laughed – should prove its mettle in a national emergency, but so it was, to the amusement of some and to the amazement of others.

Early in 1943 Utility furniture was on the market, at reasonable prices and not subject to Purchase Tax. Gordon Russell summed up the reaction:

> The intelligentia criticised it as being too conservative, the trade as being too advanced, but I was encouraged to find shots coming from both directions: it looked as if we were about right.

And indeed they were. The furniture provided was an enormous improvement on what most people had had before. A fine educational job was done in encouraging a familiarity with simple designs and Utility furniture will certainly go down as a milestone in the history of English furniture.

Post-war Furniture

When the standard of design falls as low as it did at the beginning of this century, it takes a long time to raise it. As we have seen, Utility furniture set a good standard and this was, on the whole, maintained after the war, although a number of the poorer manufacturers tried to put the clock back and sell pretentious imitations of mock-period styles.

The 'Britain Can Make It' Exhibition of 1946 was a tonic for the public at a dark time, a stimulus to industry, and an opportunity for designers to develop ideas that had been in cold storage since 1939. Except for the Ernest Race chair, whose tapering aluminium legs set a new trend, the actual furniture shown at the Exhibition was not remarkable, but the standard of display helped to tune the eyes of the public to new colours, new shapes, and new domestic arrangements. The Exhibition was the first public effort of the Council of Industrial Design, which had been established by the Board of Trade in 1944 to promote the improvement of design in British products, and which has done so much, ever since, to encourage and foster good design in this country.

During the '50s and '60s, many changes swept through the design world and these, of course, affected furniture, but it is sobering to realise that the pre-*first*-World-War work of Marcel

Breuer, Mies van der Rohe, and Alvar Aalto is only now beginning to exert any real influence in this country! Not many would believe that the chair on page 149 was made forty-one years ago.

The Festival of Britain, held on the South Bank in London in 1951, to commemorate the centenary of the Great Exhibition of 1851, was a milestone in British design. This festival of the arts, science, and industry suddenly and brilliantly gave us all a vision of a brighter, better world. Ernest Race's elegant white-painted 'Antelope' chairs were used throughout the South Bank area and helped to launch an angular, spiky look which persisted in furniture legs and lamp-stands with 'blobs' on their feet, for the next ten years.

In the mid '50s American furniture design began to have a strong influence in England. The Charles Eames and Eero Saarinen glass-fibre and moulded plastic pedestal-chairs set an entirely new standard of simplicity and integrity.

The Design Centre, in London, was opened in 1956 and has since then been a popular success, with its invitation to 'look before you shop'. Attendances there and at the Design Centre in Glasgow, have been high from the start and a growing number of people like to keep their eye both on the Centres and on the *Design Index* – an illustrated catalogue of well-designed things – so as to see what is best among British products in current production. Although poor furniture is still produced in this country there is now a wider range of well-designed pieces to choose from than at any time during the past century.

Simplicity has become the idiom of modern design, but we need to remember that furniture-designers give as much care and thought to choosing timber, fittings, and handles, and to the spacing and relationship of keyholes, handles, and hinges, as the best hand craftsmen have always done.

Furniture today is increasingly informal and adaptable and often becomes part of the architecture of a home. Room-dividers, wall storage units, stacking stools and chairs, and bed-settees, are all welcome help to those living in small homes, and where rooms have to be used for a number of purposes. Built-in furniture, pioneered in the '30s, is now accepted as normal in many rooms, and makes moving house much easier. Unit furniture, which can be added to as the need arises is another pre-war idea which is increasingly popular, and has obvious advantages. Knock-down furniture, flat-packed and delivered ready for rapid assembly, saves transport costs and enables the buyer to play an active part in furnishing his home.

The new science of ergonomics is helping furniture-designers to avoid some of the inhuman proportions of pre-war chairs, and today all furniture is lighter to look at and to use. 'Instant', inflatable chairs in expanded polyurethane foam are adaptable to a degree unknown when wood always formed the structure of a seat; chairs suspended from the ceiling on giant coil springs, or foam cushions on the floor – all these are new, and entirely in tune with the thinking and feeling of the young of today.

Transience, and obsolescence, are concepts that divide the generations more markedly than anything else. The young like movement, speed, and change; their parents and grandparents, on the other hand, tend to be obsessed with a need for durability and permanence.

A concern for durability has a period flavour and is connected with slow, pre-industrial production, with the speed of horse and sailing-ship rather than that of space travel. Long life is only one quality among many others in an object, and it is not necessarily, at all periods, a desirable one. It mattered more when things were hand-made and 'hands' worked slowly; obsolescence is inevitable and perhaps desirable in an age of speed and potential superfluity and overpopulation.

In past centuries fine, durable things were available to wealthy people, but others had to manage largely with what they could make themselves. Today, modern production can supply things of quality for everybody. Because of new opportunities, because of the housewife's growing emancipation, and because of the character of the machine itself, the best furniture of the future will inevitably be simple. Our problem is to learn to choose wisely among the enormous variety of goods available.

61 'Quasar' inflatable P.V.C. chair designed by Quasar Khan in 1967. In an age of quickly changing fashion, it is not made to last, but can be cheaply and quickly replaced when obsolete or worn out. It is easy to transport, light, and adaptable – a typical result of today's methods of production and use of new synthetic materials – and reflects, too, the informal and highly mobile life of the twentieth century

Some Technical Terms

Acanthus	Conventionalised leaf, often used as carved decoration on eighteenth-century furniture.
Apron	Ornamental rail connecting the upper parts of legs on chairs, tables, and bureaux.
Arcading	Series of arches on pillars carved on panels, especially in the early seventeenth century.
Baluster	Turned column, often twisted, tapered, or vase-shaped.
Banding	A strip, or band, of contrasting inlay, usually at the edge of a panel or round the front of a drawer.
Bentwood	Wood steamed and bent to form chair frames. This process was first developed by Thonet in Austria in the early nineteenth century, and is much used in modern furniture.
Blockboard	Modern furniture material, made of a core of wood strips covered with thick veneers.
Cartouche	Oval tablet, with a scrolled edge, often found in the centre of the pediment in early eighteenth-century cabinets or bookcases.
Chipboard	An inexpensive material made of wood chips bonded under pressure with glue.
Chip Carving	Shallow decoration on early oak furniture, cut with a chisel and gouge.
Dresser	Tiers of shelves or 'cup-boards', on which to display well-dressed rows of flagons and plate.
Ebonised	Wood painted or stained black in imitation of ebony.
Fielded panel	A raised panel with bevelled edges.
Finial	A knob ornament, turned or carved, used in the seventeenth century on intersections of stretchers, also on tops of cabinets, clock cases, and pole screens.
Fluting	Concave grooves, cut vertically on columns, pilasters, legs, etc.
Gesso	A mixture of chalk and size applied to furniture as a base for silvering or gilding.
Hutch	A box on legs with doors opening in front. The word survives in 'rabbit hutch'.
Intarsia	Pictures in perspective, made in marquetry.
Laminated	Built up from layers of the same material, e.g. plywood.
Lunette	Decoration of half-moon shape, often carved on oak furniture, and painted or inlaid in the Adam period.
Mullion	Vertical member of a window, generally stone or wood.
Ormolu	Gilded metal used for furniture mounts.
Oyster pieces	Small veneers of walnut or olive, cut transversely from branches and used in marquetry from 1660.
Pilaster	A rectangular column applied to a wall or to the front of a piece of furniture.
Plywood	Board built up from an uneven number of veneers glued together, each with the grain at right angles to the next.
Quarter cut	Method of cutting to get a well-figured grain. The log is quartered and each quarter sawn from the centre to the outer edge.
Reeding	Convex raised ornament, the opposite of fluting.
Side chair	Chair without arms.
Strapwork	Interlaced, carved, geometrically shaped bands on furniture after 1550. Of Flemish origin.
Stucco	Smooth, hard plaster, fashionable in the seventeenth and eighteenth centuries, for both inside and outside walls.
Tambour	A roll-front or shutter, made of narrow strips of wood glued to a canvas backing. Used for desks in the late eighteenth century.
Wainscot	Originally used, in the Middle Ages, to describe any imported wood suitable for making 'wains' (wagons). The meaning changed to cover wood for furniture and panelling and the word now usually applies to the short panel of wood at the floor-level of an inside wall.

A List of Books

1 SOME BOOKS WRITTEN BEFORE 1500

The Babees Book. Medieval manners for the Young: Done into modern English from Dr Furnivall's texts by Edith Rickert. (London and New York, 1908)
Chronicles by Jean Froissart. Adapted by H. P. Dunster, edited by E. Rhys. (Everyman Library, London 1906)
The Canterbury Tales by Geoffrey Chaucer. Edited by A. C. Cawley. (Everyman Library, London and New York, 1958)
De Proprietatibus by Bartholomaeus Anglicus. (Cologne, 1472?)
Utopia by Thomas More. Translated by Ralph Robinson. (Everyman Library, London and New York, 1951)

SOME EXTRACTS FROM LATE MEDIEVAL SOURCES

The Paston Letters. Edited by John Fenn and Mrs Archer-Hind. (Everyman Library, London and New York, 1924)
The Cely Papers. Selections from the correspondence and memoranda of the Cely family, Merchants of the Staple, AD 1475–1488. Edited by Henry Elliot Malden. (London, 1900)
The Stonor Letters and Papers 1290–1483. Edited by C. L. Kingsford. (2 vols., London, 1919)
Picture Source Book for Social History: From the Conquest to the Wars of the Roses. Edited by Molly Harrison and A. A. M. Wells. (London, 1958)

SOME BOOKS ABOUT LATE MEDIEVAL ENGLAND

Life and Work of the People of England by Dorothy R. Hartley and Margaret M. V. Elliott. (6 vols., London, 1925–31)
English Life in the Middle Ages by L. F. Salzman. (London, 1926)
Medieval People by Eileen Power. (10th edition, London, 1963)
Life on the English Manor by H. S. Bennett. (Cambridge, 1937)

THESE MORE GENERAL BOOKS HAVE SECTIONS ON THIS PERIOD

The Pattern of English Building by Alec Clifton-Taylor. (London, 1962)
The English Home by D. Yarwood. (London, 1956)
The Dictionary of English Furniture by Percy MacQuoid and H. C. R. Edwards. (2nd edition, 3 vols., London, 1954)

2 SOME BOOKS WRITTEN IN THE SIXTEENTH CENTURY

Extracts from Travels in England, 1598, by Paul Hentzner. Translated from the Latin in *England as seen by Foreigners in the days of Elizabeth and James the First* by W. B. Rye. (London, 1865)
The Description of England by William Harrison. Edited by G. Edelen. (Ithaca and London, 1968)
Delightes for Ladies by Sir Hugh Platt. Edited by G. E. and K. R. Fussell. (London, 1948)
The Scholemaster by Roger Ascham. Edited by L. V. Ryan. (Ithaca and London, 1968)

SOME EXTRACTS FROM SIXTEENTH-CENTURY SOURCES

The Elizabethan Home. Discovered in two dialogues by Claudius Hollyband and Peter Erondell by Claude de Sainliens. Edited by M. Saint-Clare-Byrne. (Revised edition, London, 1949)
They Saw it Happen, 1485–1688. Edited by C. R. N. Routh. (Oxford, 1956)
How They Lived: Tudors and Stuarts. Edited by Molly Harrison and O. M. Royston. (Oxford, 1963)
Picture Source Book for Social History: The Sixteenth Century. Edited by Molly Harrison and M. E. Bryant. (London, 1951)
The Oxford Book of Sixteenth-Century Verse. Chosen by Sir E. K. Chambers. (Oxford, editions since 1932)

SOME BOOKS ABOUT THE SIXTEENTH CENTURY

Life and Work of the People of England by D. R. Hartley and M. M. V. Elliott

Costume of the Western World. Edited by James Laver. (6 vols., London, 1951-)
    Early Tudor by James Laver
    Elizabethan and Jacobean by G. Reynolds
The Connoisseur Period Guides to the houses, decoration, furnishing and chattels of the classic periods by Herbert C. R. Edwards and L. G. G. Ramsey. (6 vols., London, 1956-58)
Tudor Family Portrait by B. Winchester. (London, 1955)
The Elizabethans at Home by Elizabeth Burton. (London, 1967)
Life in Tudor England by Penry Williams. (London and New York, 1964)
Life in Elizabethan England by A. H. Dodd. (London, 1961)

THESE MORE GENERAL BOOKS HAVE SECTIONS ON THIS PERIOD

Houses by M. and A. Potter. (London, 1947)
Interiors by M. and A. Potter. (London, 1957)
English Furniture Styles by R. Fastnedge. (London, 1962)
Furniture: An Explanatory History by D. Reeves. (2nd edition, London, 1959)

3   SOME BOOKS WRITTEN IN THE SEVENTEENTH CENTURY

The Journeys of Celia Fiennes. Edited by Christopher Morris. (London, 1949)
Farewell to Husbandry by Gervase Markham. (London, 1620)
The Letters of Dorothy Osborne to William Temple. Edited by G. C. Moore Smith. (Oxford, 1928)
Memoirs of the Verney Family during the Seventeenth Century. Edited by Frances Lady Verney and Margaret Lady Verney. (2nd edition, 2 vols., London, 1904)

SOME EXTRACTS FROM SEVENTEENTH-CENTURY SOURCES

They Saw it Happen. An anthology of eye-witnesses' accounts of events in British history, 1689-1897. Edited by T. Charles-Edwards and B. Richardson. (Oxford, 1958)
Picture Source Book for Social History: The Seventeenth Century. Edited by Molly Harrison and A. A. M. Wells. (London, 1953)
The Oxford Book of Seventeenth-Century Verse. Chosen by Sir H. J. C. Grierson and C. Bullough. (Oxford, editions since 1934)

SOME BOOKS ABOUT THE SEVENTEENTH CENTURY

The Connoisseur Period Guide
Life in a Noble Household by G. Scott-Thomson. (London, 1937)
Life and Work of the People of England by D. R. Hartley and M. M. V. Elliott

THESE MORE GENERAL BOOKS HAVE SECTIONS ON THIS PERIOD

Looking at Furniture by Sir Gordon Russell. (London, 1964)
English Home Life through the Ages by C. Hole. (2nd edition, London, 1949)
Early Conversation Pictures from the Middle Ages to about 1730. A study in origins by Herbert C. R. Edwards. (London, 1954)
Houses by M. and A. Potter
Interiors by M. and A. Potter
The Englishman's Food by J. C. Drummond and Anne Wilbraham. (London, 1939)

4   SOME BOOKS WRITTEN IN THE EIGHTEENTH CENTURY

Memoirs of Dr. Burney by Mme d'Arblay (Fanny Burney). (3 vols., London, 1832)
The Vicar of Wakefield by Oliver Goldsmith. (Everyman Library, London and New York, 1956)
The Diary of a Country Parson by James Woodforde. Edited by J. Beresford. (World's Classics, London, 1949-)
The Art of Cookery Made Plain and Easy by Hannah Glasse. (Numerous editions, London and Edinburgh, from 1747)

SOME EXTRACTS FROM EIGHTEENTH-CENTURY SOURCES

They Saw it Happen, 1689-1897. Edited by T. Charles-Edwards and B. Richardson
Picture Source Book for Social History: The Eighteenth Century. Edited by Molly Harrison and A. A. M. Wells. (London, 1955)

Verney Letters of the Eighteenth Century from the MSS at Claydon House. Edited by Margaret Lady Verney. (2 vols., London, 1930)
Blundell's Diary and Letter Book 1702–1728. Edited by Margaret Blundell. (Liverpool, 1952)
The Purefoy Letters. Letters written by Elizabeth and Henry Purefoy, 1735–1753. Edited by G. Eland. (2 vols., London, 1931)

SOME BOOKS ABOUT THE EIGHTEENTH CENTURY

Life and Work of the People of England by D. R. Hartley and M. M. V. Elliott
The Connoisseur Period Guide
Georgian Grace by John Gloag. (Feltham, 1967)
Housekeeping in the Eighteenth Century by Rosamond Bayne Powell. (London, 1956)

THESE MORE GENERAL BOOKS HAVE SECTIONS ON THIS PERIOD

Houses by M. and A. Potter
Interiors by M. and A. Potter
Homes by Molly Harrison. (London, 1960)
The English Home by D. Yarwood

5 SOME BOOKS WRITTEN IN THE NINETEENTH CENTURY

Hints on Household Taste in Furniture, Upholstery and other details by Sir Charles Lock Eastlake. (London, 1868)
Letters of Queen Victoria: 1837–61. Edited by A. C. Benson and Viscount Esher. (London, 1907)
    1862–85. Edited by G. E. Buckle. (London, 1926–28)
    1886–1901. Edited by G. E. Buckle. (London, 1930–32)
Memoirs 1814–1860 by Charles Greville. Edited by Lytton Strachey and Roger Fulford. (8 vols., London, 1938)
Lives of the Engineers by Samuel Smiles. (New impression, 3 vols., Newton Abbot, 1968)

SOME EXTRACTS FROM NINETEENTH-CENTURY SOURCES

They Saw it Happen, 1689–1897. Edited by T. Charles-Edwards and B. Richardson
Picture Source Book for Social History: The Early Nineteenth Century. Edited by Molly Harrison and A. A. M. Wells (London, 1957)
Picture Source Book for Social History: The Late Nineteenth Century. Edited by Molly Harrison and O. M. Royston. (London, 1961)

SOME BOOKS ABOUT THE NINETEENTH CENTURY

The Connoisseur Period Guide
Victorian Comfort by John Gloag. (London, 1961)
The Victorian Home. Some aspects of nineteenth-century taste and manners by Ralph Dutton. (London, 1954)
Victorian Panorama. A survey of life and fashion from contemporary photographs by Peter Quennell. (London, 1937)
Life in Victorian England by W. J. Reader. (London, 1964)
Pioneers in Modern Design, from William Morris to Walter Gropius by Nikolaus Pevsner. (Harmondsworth, 1960)
The Aesthetic Movement: prelude to Art Nouveau by Elizabeth Aslin. (London, 1969)

THESE MORE GENERAL BOOKS HAVE SECTIONS ON THIS PERIOD

Looking at Furniture by Sir Gordon Russell
A Picture History of the English Home by R. Furneaux Jordan. (London, 1959)
Homes by Molly Harrison
The English Home by D. Yarwood

6 SOME BOOKS DEALING WITH FURNITURE IN THE TWENTIETH CENTURY

The Modern House in England by F. R. S. Yorke. (London, 1957)
The House, a Machine for Living In by Anthony Bertram. (London, 1935)
Life since 1900 by Charles Furth. (London, 1966)
A Picture History of Furniture by Frank Davis. (London, 1958)

Furniture Design Set Free: the British furniture revolution from 1851 to the present day by David Joel. (London, 1969)
Pioneers of Modern Design by Nikolaus Pevsner
The Decorative Twenties by Martin Battersby. (London, 1969)

THESE MAGAZINES ARE ALSO USEFUL

House and Garden
Homes and Gardens
House Beautiful (now incorporated with *Good Housekeeping*)
The Architectural Review
Design
Which?

All are published in London

Acknowledgements

THE AUTHOR AND PUBLISHERS wish to record their grateful thanks to copyright owners for the use of the illustrations listed below:
Art Gallery and Temple Newsam House, Leeds for: 40
Ashmolean Museum, Oxford for: 34
Bodleian Library, Oxford for: title-page, 4
British Museum for: 6, 8, 11
The Carpenters Company for: 12
The Council of Industrial Design for: 54, 59
The Courtauld Institute for: 21, 31
John Crane (*Colonial Williamsburg*) for: 36
Desbrow Public Relations for: 2
Glasgow Art Gallery (Burrell Collection) for: 16
Harris Museum and Art Gallery, Preston for: 48
Ipswich Museum Committee for: 18
Leonard Koetser Gallery for: 22
The Mansell Collection for: 10, 20, 51
The National Gallery for: 7, 26
The National Gallery of Ireland for: 33
National Museum of Wales, Welsh Folk Museum for: 14, 19
The National Trust for: 23
The National Trust and A. F. Kersting for: 37, 44
Old Master Galleries (Wengraf) Ltd for: 13
Radio Times Hulton Picture Library for: 5, 9, 41, 42, 46, 47, 49, 50, 56, 57, 60
R.I.B.A. for: 55
Gordon Russell Ltd for: 58
Sotheby & Co. for: 32
Stadelsinstitut, Frankfurt for: 17
Dr J. F. Stent for: 28
L. and M. Taylor Ltd for: 1, 15
Ultralite International Ltd for: 61
Victoria and Albert Museum for: 3, 24, 25, 27, 29, 30, 35, 38, 39, 43, 45, 52, 53

Index

Page numbers given in italics refer to illustrations

Ackerman, Rudolph, *The Repository of the Arts*, 106, 114
Adam, the brothers, 73
  Robert, 81, *83*, 90, 94, 97
Aken, Joseph van, *Saying Grace*, 74
American cabinet-makers, 79, *80*
American influence, 151
Art in Industry Exhibition (1935), 147
Art Journal Catalogue, 127
Art Nouveau, *133*, 136
Arts and Crafts Exhibition Society, 112, 143
Artworkers' Guild, the, 112, 122
Austen, Jane, *Mansfield Park*, 114

Babees Book, 24
Barnsley,
  Edward, 143
  Ernest, 117, 142
  Sidney, 117, 142
Bauhaus, the, 134, 138, 146
Beds, 13, *13*, *19*, 22–4, 35–7, 65–6, 92–6, 125–27
  box, 23
  couch-beds, 93
  divans, 147
  four-poster, 35, 65, 92
  Garrick's, *95*
  Great Bed of Ware, 36
  half-tester, 93
  state, 93
  truckle, 23, *35*, 36
Beech, use of, 57
Beeton, Mrs, *Book of Household Management*, 123
Bolsover, Thomas, 85
Boswell, James, *London Journal*, 92
Boulle, André-Charles, 63, 119
Boulle (boule, buhl), 63–4, 119
Breuer, Marcel, 134, 135, 145, 146, 151
'Britain Can Make It' Exhibition (1946), 150
British Empire Exhibition at Wembley, 137
Brown, 'Capability', 73
Brueghel, Pieter, the Younger, *32*
Buhl, *see* boulle
Building, 29–30, 49–50, 72–3, 102–5, 130–35
Bullock, George, 119
Burney, Fanny, 118

Canework, *50*, 56, *57*, *63*, *67*, 96

Carlyle, Mrs, Thomas, 114, 126
Chermayeff, Serge, 135
Chinese influence, 78–9, *95*, 107, 113
Chippendale, Thomas, 78–9
  Gentleman and Cabinet-Maker's Director, 78, 79, 83
Chippendale, Thomas, the Younger, 113
Christening of a Prince or Princess, The, 24
Classical influence, 113
Clocks, 67–8, *84*
Cobbett, William, 81, 119, 125
Cooking utensils, 22
Coques, Gonzales, *A Family Group*, *58*
Council of Industrial Design, 150
Cradles, 24, *32*, 36, *50*, 96, 127
Crafts Centre of Great Britain, 144
Crafts Council of Great Britain, 144
Crane, Walter, 116, 136
Cullen, James, 94

Defoe, Daniel, *The Compleat English Tradesman*, 90
Delaney, Mrs, 84
Design Centre, the, 151
Design Index, the, 151
Design and Industries Association, 145
  Exhibition (1933), 147
Dickens, Charles, 104, 122
Domestic conditions, 9, 11–13, 20, *22*, 31–2, 69, 73, 74–5, 95–6, 98, 104, 106–8, *109*, 120, *124*, 125–27, 131
Draughts, game of, *16*

Edgeworth, Maria, 119
Egyptian influence, 137
Erasmus, 32, 34
Evelyn, John, 57, 61, 67
Eworth, Hans, *47*
Eyck, Jan Van, *19*

Festival of Britain, 1951, the, 151
Fiennes, Celia, *Tour Through England on a Side Saddle*, 62, 67, 93
Floor coverings,
  carpets, *19*, 34, 51–2
  rush matting, *25*, 51
  rushes, 20, 33
French influence, 106
French polishing, 119
Fry, Maxwell, 135

Furnishings, 19, 24–5, 52, 55, 65–6, 67, *89*, 90, 105
Furniture Gazette of 1875, 111

Gill, Eric, 143
Gillow (the firm of), 123
Gimson, Ernest, 117, 142, 145
Go-cart, 58, *58*
Godwin, E. W., 122
Goldsmith, Oliver, *The Vicar of Wakefield*, 89
  The Deserted Village, 99
Gostelowe, Jonathan, 79
  Journeyman's Philadelphia Book of Prices, 79
Gothic revival influence, 121
Great Exhibition, 1851, the, 109, 127
Gropius, Walter, 134, 135

Hand-made furniture, 142–44
Hardy, F. D., *124*
Harrison, William, 30, 33, 35, 47
Heal, Sir Ambrose, 144
  The London Furniture Makers 1660–1840, 79
Hepplewhite, George, 79
Holkham Bible Picture Book, 15
Honneurs de la Cour, Les, 17
Howard, Ebenezer, *Garden Cities of Tomorrow*, 131
Huguenots in England, 63
Hygiene, standards of, 95–6

Inlay, 45, 47, 62
Italian influence, 33

Japanese influence, 122–23
Japanning and Varnishing, A Treatise on, 65, *see also* Lacquering
Jones, Inigo, 50, 72

Kauffmann, Angelica, 73
Khan, Quasar, *153*
Knock-down furniture, 152

Lacquering, *64*, 64–5, 113
Lancaster, Osbert, 132
Latex foam rubber, 147
'Le Corbusier', 134, 138
Lemmius, Dr Levinus, 31–2
London Trades Directory, 111
Lubetkin, Berthold, 135
Lutyens, Sir Edwin, 132

Mackintosh, Charles Rennie, 132
Mahogany, import and use of, 75–6, *77*, 82

Marquetry, 9, 46, 62, 63
Mattresses, 22, 23, 25, 36, 37, 94
Mendelsohn, Erich, 135
Mitford, Mary Russell, *Our Village*, 107
More, Sir Thomas, 45
Moreau, Gustave, *92*
Morris, William, 110–12, 117, 122, 127, 144
Mortimer, Raymond, 140

Nash, John, 107

Oetzmann & Co., *128*
Oriental influence, 64

Palladian style, 72–3
Papiermâché used in furniture, 114, 117, 127
Paris Exhibition of 1925, 137
Patient Countess, The, 42
Pevsner, Dr Nikolaus, 148
Philipps, Fabian, 68–9
Pope, Alexander, 74
Post-war furniture, 150–52
Pre-Raphaelite Brotherhood, 110, 122
Public Health Act (1875), 105
Pugin, Augustus, *121*

Race, Ernest, 150, 151
Regency furniture, 112–15
Reinagle, *Mrs Congreve and her Daughters*, *71*
Reproduction furniture, 139–42, *141*
Rhodes, Hugh, *The Book of Nurture*, 36
Rohe, Mies van der, 134, 146, *149*, 151
Rooms, 31–2, 51–2, 73–6, 105–12, 135–38
Royal Society, the, 49
Ruskin, John, 103, 110
Russell, Sir Gordon, 119, 140, *141*, 145, 148–50
Russell, John, *Boke of Nurture*, 20
Russell, R. D., *141*

Satinwood, import and use of, 85, 88
Seating, 17–18, 40–4, 52–9, 77–82, 112–17
  baby chairs, *32*, *40*
  Barcelona chair, 146, *149*
  benches, 18, *44*
  box chairs, 41, 42
  built-in, *13*, 17, *27*
  caquetoire (or gossip) chairs, 44
  chaises-longues, 114
  Charles II chair, *63*
  Chippendale chair, 55
  couches, 55–6, *57*

Seating (*continued*)
  day-beds, 56, *57*
  farthingale chair, 42
  high chairs, 58
  inflatable chairs, 152, *153*
  library chair, *100*
  Ottomans, 114, *115*
  Regency chairs, 112–15, *115*
  settees, 147
  settles, *10*, *16*, 18, *22*, *32*, 58–9
  sofas, 114–15
  stools, *13*, 18, *22*, *25*, 40, 42
  upholstered chairs, 52, *53*, *54*, 55, *67*, 115–16
  'Vassily' chair, 146
  William and Mary chair, *63*
  window-seats, 17, *27*
  Windsor chairs, 18, 82
  X-shaped chairs, 18, *53*, 55
Shaw, Norman, 132
Sheraton, Thomas,
  Cabinet Dictionary, 117, 123
  Cabinet Directory, 127
  Drawing Book, 99
Simond, L., *Journal of a Tour in Great Britain*, 106
Smith, Adam, 82
Smith, George, *Household Furniture*, 120
Southall, J., *A Treatise of Buggs*, 96
Speer, John, 94
Storage, 14–17, 38–40, 59–65, 96–9, 120–27
  aumbry, 16
  bookcases, 62, 98, *118*, 124
  buffets, 17, 21, 62
  built-in cupboards, 146
  bureau-bookcases, 62, 98
  canterbury, 123
  chests (and coffers), 14–15, *16*, *16*, *26*, *37*, 38–40, 46, 60
  chests-of-drawers, 40, 60, 97
  chiffoniers, 120
  china cabinets, 61, *80*, 122
  commodes, 98
  cupboards, 16, *16*, 17, *21*, 38–9, *39*, 61, 62, 146
  dressers, 17, 99
  'Dressing buroes', 98
  lacquer cabinet, *64*
  marquetry cabinet, *9*
  sideboards, 17, 99
  tallboys, 61, 97
  wardrobes, 146
  whatnots, 122
Strapwork, 46
Strawberry Hill library, *91*
Stubbes, Ralph, *An Anatomie of Abuses*, 45
Swedish Decorative Art Exhibition, 146
Swift, Jonathan, 92

Tables 20–22, *44*, 44–5, 66–7, 82–91, 117–20
  card, 88
  china, 86
  circular, 82, 117
  claw, 82
  console, 84
  dining, 85, 117
  dressing, *84*, 90
  drop-leaf, 45
  extending (or 'drawing'), 45
  gate-leg (or falling), 66
  library, 88
  occasional, 117
  Pembroke, 88
  pier, 67, 85
  pillar and claw, 82–3
Table-ware, 20, *21*, *47*, *74*, 85
Tea drinking, 85–7, *109*
Torrigiano, Pietro, 33
Town and Country Planning Act (1947), 135
Trapnell, C., 111, 125
Trusler, *Domestic Management*, 87
Tubular steel furniture, 145–46
Tusser, Thomas, *Five Hundred Points of Good Husbandrie*, 16

Unit furniture, 147, 151–52
Utility Furniture, 148–50, *149*

Veneering, 60, 122
Victoria and Albert Museum, 36, 46, *95*, 136
Voysey, C. F. A., 117, 132, *133*, 139, 142

Walnut, import and use of, 57, 59, *63*, 76, 78
Webster, Thomas, *A Tea Party*, 109
Wedgwood, Josiah, 85
Wells, H. G., 130, 131
Whatman, Susanna, *Housekeeping Book*, 86–7
Whitehead, William, 78
Wilde, Oscar, 110
Wilson, Benjamin, *89*
Woodforde, Parson, 90, 95
Wren, Sir Christopher, 72
Wright, Frank Lloyd, *Manifesto on Art and the Machine*, 134
Wright, Joseph ('Wright of Derby'), 81
Writing,
  bureaux, 62, 98
  Davenport desks, 123
  desks, 26, 27
  scriptoires, 62
  slope, 25
  tables, 25, 25–6, 27

Young Childrens Book, The, 34

Printed in Great Britain by Jarrold & Sons Limited, Norwich